EUREKA!

THE MOST AMAZING
SCIENTIFIC DISCOVERIES
OF ALL TIME

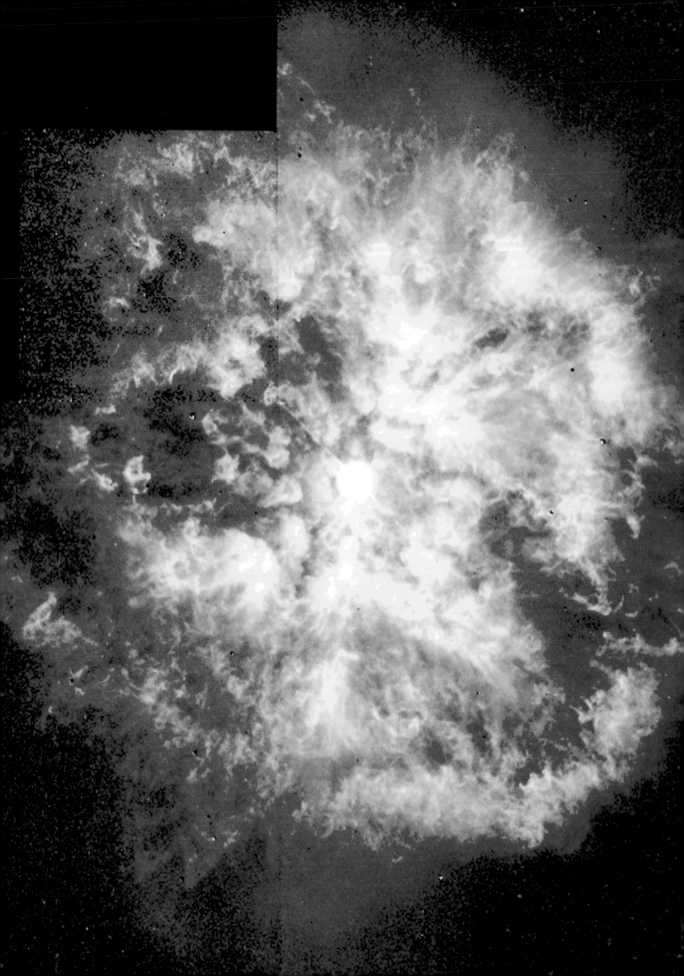

Dr. MIKE GOLDSMITH

EUREKA!

THE MOST AMAZING
SCIENTIFIC DISCOVERIES
OF ALL TIME

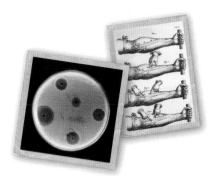

CONTENTS

SCIENTIFIC DISCOVERIES

▶▶ Science allows humans to understand the world. Over many centuries, thousands of scientists have discovered and invented all kinds of things. Here are a few of their greatest moments of discovery. As Archimedes said, after working out a special way of measuring, *Eureka!*

KEY TO TIMELINE
• The color tells you what the discovery was about.
• Remember that there is a glossary on page 94 if you find a word difficult.

 MEDICINE

 HUMAN BODY

 MATTER AND ENERGY

 PLANET EARTH

 THE UNIVERSE

	c. 440 BCE	**Democritus** suggests the existence of atoms, which are one of the smallest units of matter in the universe.
	c. 350 BCE	**Aristotle** classifies, or groups, most of the animals known at the time.
	c. 240 BCE	**Eratosthenes** works out the size of the Earth.
	c. 213 BCE	**Archimedes** uses his discoveries in science to build war machines.
	132	**Zhang Heng** invents an instrument for detecting, or picking up, earthquakes.
	1025	**Avicenna** makes a complete guide to medicine.
1500s →	**1543**	**Nicolaus Copernicus** publishes his theory that the Earth goes around the Sun.
	1572	**Tycho Brahe** discovers a supernova, which is an exploding star.
1600s →	**1600**	**William Gilbert** proves that the Earth acts like a magnet.
	1609	**Galileo Galilei** observes moons through a telescope and proves that the Earth goes around the Sun.
	1609	**Johannes Kepler** proves that the planets go around the Sun in oval-shaped paths called orbits.
	1628	**William Harvey** proves that the heart pumps blood around the body.
	1656	**Christiaan Huygens** discovers rings around the planet Saturn.
	1673	**Antonie van Leeuwenhoek** discovers microorganisms, which are tiny life forms.
	1687	**Isaac Newton** works out his laws of gravity, the force that holds you to Earth, and motion, also known as movement.
1700s →	**1735**	**Carl Linnaeus** works out a way to group and name all living things.
	1772	**Antoine Lavoisier** shows that oxygen is needed for breathing and for burning things.
	1781	**William Herschel** discovers the planet Uranus.
	1785	**James Hutton** establishes geology, which is the study of the Earth, as a proper science.
	1791	**Pierre-Simon de Laplace** builds a mathematical model of the solar system.
1800s →	**1808**	**John Dalton** invents modern atomic theory based on the idea that all matter is made up of atoms.
	1831	**Michael Faraday** invents the electric motor and the dynamo.
	1842	**Richard Owen** comes up with the name 'dinosaur' for a group of reptiles that are no longer living.
	1859	**Charles Darwin** publishes his theory of evolution, which explains how species change gradually over time.
	1859	**Gustav Kirchhoff** improves our understanding of heat and light.
	1864	**James Clerk Maxwell** works out laws of magnetism and electricity.
	1865	**Claude Bernard** shows how the body works as a system.
	1865	**Gregor Mendel** studies how plants pass on different characteristics, such as flower color.

Medicine
Louis Pasteur

Human Body
Francis Crick and
James Watson

Matter and Energy
Marie Curie

Planet Earth
Charles Darwin

The Universe
Edwin Hubble

1869	**Dmitri Mendeleev** arranges elements, chemicals made up of one sort of atom, to create the Periodic Table.
1872	**Ludwig Boltzmann** publishes a mathematical theory relating particle motions to heat
1877	**Robert Koch** proves that each disease is caused by its own particular germ.
1885	**Louis Pasteur and Émile Roux** discover how to treat rabies.
1891	**Eugène Dubois** discovers the fossils of a human-like animal, which was probably our ancestor.
1895	**Wilhelm Röntgen** discovers X-rays, which allow us to see inside our bodies.
1897	**Joseph J. Thomson** discovers the electron, a tiny particle found in all atoms.
1898	**Marie and Pierre Curie** discover the elements radium and polonium, which lead to advances in medicine.
1900s → 1900	**Max Planck** discovers that energy can exist in lumps, which he called quanta.
1905	**Albert Einstein** comes up with the theory of relativity, changing the way we think about time and space.
1907	**Ernest Rutherford** shows that an atom has a tiny hard core, called a nucleus.
1912	**Alfred Wegener** suggests that Earth's big land masses, the continents, have drifted apart over millions of years.
1913	**Niels Bohr** develops a theory that explains the structure of atoms.
1925	**Erwin Schrödinger** comes up with a mathematical theory about quanta, which are lumps of energy.
1925	**Werner Heisenberg** proves that measurements of tiny objects cannot be exact.
1927	**Georges Lemaître** develops a theory, later known as the Big Bang theory, explaining the start of the universe.
1928	**Alexander Fleming** discovers penicillin, a life-saving medicine used to treat infections.
1929	**Edwin Hubble** helps prove that the universe is expanding.
1930	**Linus Pauling** discovers how atoms are bonded together.
1932	**Paul Dirac** suggests that there is a material called anti-matter, like matter, but with an opposite charge.
1939	**Otto Frisch and Lise Meitner** discover that the core of an atom can be split into smaller parts.
1942	**Enrico Fermi** builds the first nuclear reactor, helping to bring about nuclear power.
1948	**Richard Feynman** develops an accurate version of quantum theory, which looks at matter and energy.
1951	**Barbara McClintock** carries out pioneering work on genes, the instructions that make us what we are.
1953	**James Watson, Francis Crick and Rosalind Franklin** discover how DNA tells a body to grow.
1953	**Stanley Miller and Harold Urey** recreate the conditions for life in a model of the early Earth.
1955	**Jonas Salk** finds a treatment for polio, an infectious disease.
1957	**Gertrude Elion and George Hitchings** make a drug that allows doctors to transplant organs.
1964	**Murray Gell-Mann** further develops our understanding of the atom.
1965	**Arno Penzias and Robert Wilson** observe radio waves that prove the Big Bang theory.
1967	**Jocelyn Bell Burnell and Antony Hewish** discover the first pulsar, a type of star.
1974	**Stephen Hawking** proves that black holes in space 'glow', emitting a form of radiation.
1984	**Michael Green and John Schwarz** develop 'string theory'. It aims to link quantum physics and relativity.
1995	**Michel Mayor and Didier Queloz** discover the first planet traveling around a star other than our Sun.
2000s → 2003	**NASA** works out the age of the universe as being 13.7 billion years.
2013	**Takanori Takebe and colleagues** grow a working liver from single cells, the biological unit of living organisms.

SEEING THE INVISIBLE

SCIENTIFIC AIMS	▶▶ To discover and look at microscopic living things, which are creatures around us too small to see with our own eyes.
CHALLENGES ///////////////////////// Little education; his strange methods, such as breeding lice, upset people	**WHO** ANTONIE VAN LEEUWENHOEK **WHERE** Delft, the Netherlands **WHEN** 1673 to 1677 **METHOD** Made hundreds of powerful glass lenses that magnified, or enlarged, things. Leeuwenhoek kept his lens-making secret, then used the lenses to build microscopes.
RESULTS	Leeuwenhoek saw a microscopic world that no one had seen before, including tiny life forms made up of single cells. He called these single-celled life forms 'animalcules'. Today, we call them microbes.

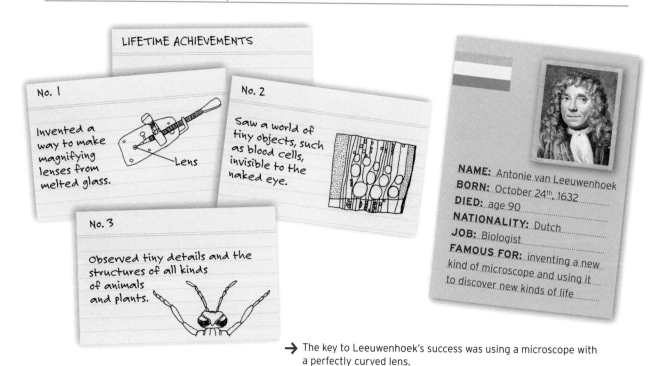

LIFETIME ACHIEVEMENTS

No. 1
Invented a way to make magnifying lenses from melted glass.
Lens

No. 2
Saw a world of tiny objects, such as blood cells, invisible to the naked eye.

No. 3
Observed tiny details and the structures of all kinds of animals and plants.

NAME: Antonie van Leeuwenhoek
BORN: October 24th, 1632
DIED: age 90
NATIONALITY: Dutch
JOB: Biologist
FAMOUS FOR: inventing a new kind of microscope and using it to discover new kinds of life

→ The key to Leeuwenhoek's success was using a microscope with a perfectly curved lens.

SEEING THE INVISIBLE

▶▶ What strange creatures had Leeuwenhoek discovered?

↑ Leeuwenhoek held his microscope close to his eye against a bright background. Getting a clear view of an object required patience, careful adjustment of the light and excellent eyesight.

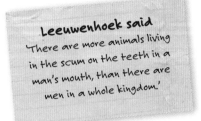

↑ This man is using a microscope as Leeuwenhoek would have done. As a trainee cloth merchant, Leeuwenhoek used to look through beads of glass to magnify cloth and judge its quality.

Delicately, Leeuwenhoek held the small brass microscope to his left eye. He closed his other eye, but all he could make out were blurred light and dark shapes. He held his breath to keep the image steady while with his other hand he felt for the focusing screw on the device. Slowly, he began to turn it. The image swam and shook, then, suddenly, it was clear and sharp. He was gazing at a new world, a world in a tiny fragment of dirt mounted on his microscope! Dozens of identical whitish objects, like short lengths of pipe, lay scattered about, and they were moving. It was a swarm of living creatures, each tinier than the head of a pin!

He was the first person to see them. Today, we call such things microbes. He called them 'animalcules'.

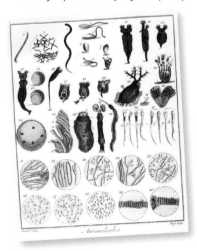

↑ Leeuwenhoek's careful drawings are so good that we can easily identify what he saw. The creatures on the top right are 'rotifers', found in rivers worldwide.

→ Today, all microscopes have several lenses – Leeuwenhoek's were more like magnifying glasses, but his skill in making the lenses meant their images were sharp and clear.

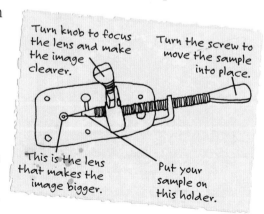

Turn knob to focus the lens and make the image clearer.

Turn the screw to move the sample into place.

This is the lens that makes the image bigger.

Put your sample on this holder.

DANGER! The flies that Leeuwenhoek enjoyed studying could carry disease. Staring through the tiny lenses could strain your eyes.

Leeuwenhoek was a cloth merchant, not a trained scientist and had no colleagues to discuss his discoveries with – he had no idea even how to publish them. In the end he wrote to the Royal Society, far away in England. After many letters, full of careful drawings of his findings, he was granted membership of the Society, and his worldwide fame began. The new science of microbiology sprang from his findings, which led to cures for many diseases and a clearer understanding of the nature of life.

Like most scientists, Leeuwenhoek was hugely curious. When he traveled to Britain in 1680, he studied the chalk cliffs on the south coast. He also studied dead bodies, and found that there were crystals in the joints of those who had suffered from gout, a disease common at the time. With his microscope he saw that the eyes of some insects are 'compound', that is, they are made of many separate lenses, all joined together. Though mocked for this at the time, he was correct.

↑ Leeuwenhoek also studied a spider he found running about his house. 'Viewing him with my microscopes, I observed that his body and legs were covered with a great number of hairs, as thick as the bristles on a hog's back.'

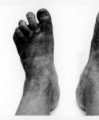

A CURE FOR A KILLER DISEASE

SCIENTIFIC AIMS	To find a vaccine that would stop the deadly disease of rabies from killing almost everything it infected.
CHALLENGES //////////////////// Risk of infection; outcry and the threat of imprisonment for using untested treatment on a child	**WHO** **LOUIS PASTEUR** along with his assistant Émile Roux **WHERE** Paris **WHEN** 1882 to 1885 **METHOD** Pasteur carried out years of painstaking research to identify the tiny organism that caused the disease. He also experimented on animals to obtain samples of the infection.
RESULTS	In the 19th century rabies was rife, and often passed on to humans through bites from infected dogs and wild animals. Louis Pasteur discovered a successful treatment.

LIFETIME ACHIEVEMENTS

No. 1
Proved that most infectious diseases are caused by tiny living things known as microorganisms.

No. 2
Created vaccines to treat the diseases of rabies, anthrax and chicken cholera.

No. 3
Developed the technique of pasteurization to remove harmful bacteria from liquids by heating.

NAME: Louis Pasteur
BORN: December 27th, 1822
DIED: age 72
NATIONALITY: French
JOB: chemist and microbiologist
FAMOUS FOR: making lives safer through his work on vaccines and pasteurization

→ A doctor injects a young French boy with the brand-new rabies vaccine. Pasteur looks on, wondering if it will work or make the patient more ill.

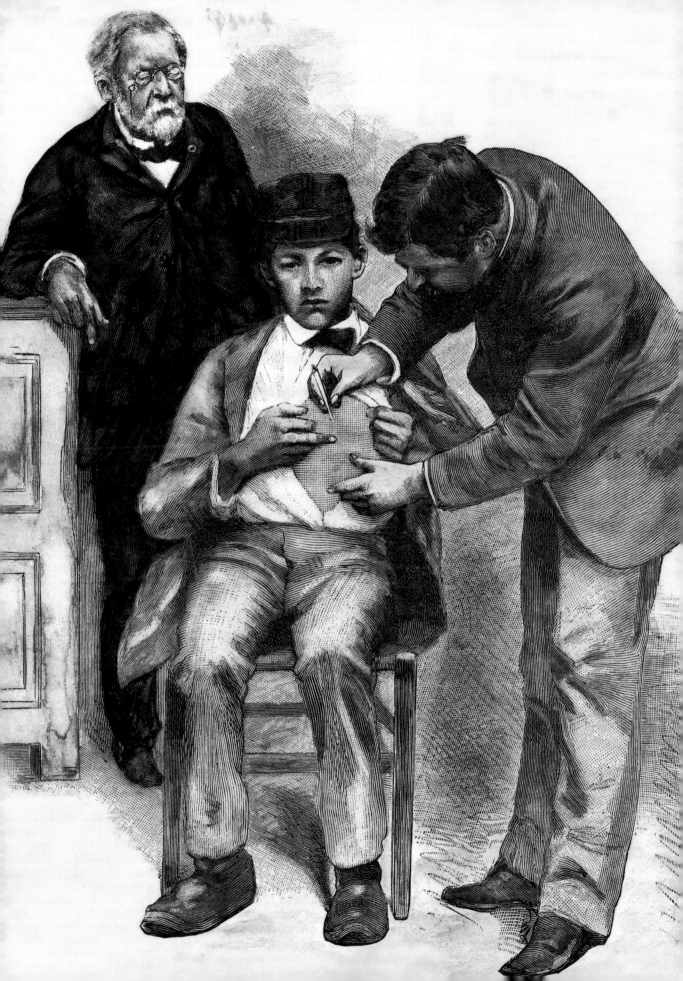

A CURE FOR A KILLER DISEASE

▶▶ Could Pasteur stop the raging rabies virus in its tracks?

On July 6th, 1885, Louis Pasteur was thrown into a life-or-death struggle. Nine-year-old Joseph Meister from Alsace, France, arrived at Pasteur's laboratory in Paris after a 250 mile journey. Two days earlier, young Joseph had been severely savaged by a rabid dog. He had been bitten a total of 14 times. Pasteur asked two French medical doctors, Alfred Vulpian and Jacques-Joseph Grancher, to see him. Both agreed that without treatment the boy could well face death.

↑ A soldier fights for his life with a rabid dog on the streets of a French town. During the 19th century, rabies killed hundreds of people in Europe.

Pasteur remembered the terrible suffering of rabies victims he had seen when he was a child. The rabies virus, which was carried in animal saliva, took several weeks to travel through the nervous system, attacking the spinal cord and brain. Victims suffered terrible shakes, fevers and spasms. They also suffered hallucinations, which means they saw things that weren't there. They found swallowing painful and eventually fell into a coma. Death followed soon after.

↑ Pasteur examines a flask of grape juice. As a young man, he started his work on microscopic living things by finding that yeast broke down sugars into alcohol in a process called fermentation.

DANGER! Pasteur sometimes drew fresh saliva from an infected dog's jaws by sucking on a tube. This was extremely risky!

↑ Pasteur studies the dogs he has tested his rabies vaccine on, checking to see if the vaccine is working and his calculations are correct.

For about three years Pasteur and his assistant Émile Roux had been experimenting with a treatment for rabies, but Pasteur felt that the work was far from complete. Although he had tested his vaccine on a handful of dogs, he had yet to try it on a human. Pasteur and his assistants had risked their own lives collecting rabid dogs and their infected drool.

Over a tense period of 10 days, Pasteur injected Joseph Meister with 13 doses of the rabies vaccine, each stronger than the one before. He waited and fretted, hoping that his treatment would work. Joseph's reaction to the vaccine would make or break Pasteur's career. Pasteur knew that scientific evidence was on his side because rabies wasn't the first deadly disease he had investigated. In 1877, anthrax, a lethal virus that killed thousands of sheep, had swept through Europe. This was when he started thinking about how to save lives.

↑ Pasteur's high-powered microscope allowed him to investigate bacteria, which are organisms that can cause disease. He identified different types of bacteria and looked at how to stop those that caused life-threatening diseases.

A CURE FOR A KILLER DISEASE

▶▶ Could Pasteur stop the raging rabies virus in its tracks?

↑ Louis Pasteur works in his laboratory. Germs could easily ruin his experiments, so he insisted that his laboratory was always spotlessly clean.

↑ The glass jar on the left contains the spinal cord of a rabbit infected with the rabies virus. Pasteur weakened the virus by exposing it to the air before injecting patients.

Anthrax could infect and kill humans as well as sheep. Through his experiments, Pasteur found that he could create a weakened form of the disease. When he injected it into sheep, their bodies produced substances to fight the disease successfully. This is a vaccine. In 1881, Pasteur injected a herd of sheep with his new anthrax vaccine.

↑ Pasteur treats sheep infected with anthrax. Within 10 years, half a million cows and 3.5 million sheep had been protected against the disease.

Twenty days later, he infected these animals and another group of unvaccinated animals with full-strength anthrax. All those animals that had not received Pasteur's vaccine died. All those that had received his treatment lived. Pasteur was using this experience to create his rabies vaccine. In the laboratory, he discovered that parts of rabid rabbits produced a far weaker version of the virus.

LOUIS PASTEUR
At age 20, Pasteur failed his science exams twice! He still went on to make a series of stunning breakthroughs in science and medicine.

1848	1859	1863	1865
Makes major advance in understanding the structure of molecules in crystals.	Proves that life cannot grow in plain air with prize-winning experiment.	Discovers how microbes contaminate wine and how spoiling can be prevented by heating.	Discovers two types of bacteria causing disease in silkworms. Helps save the French silk industry.

Two of Pasteur's assistants work on producing vaccines. Once a successful vaccine was created, large quantities were needed to treat infected people and animals.

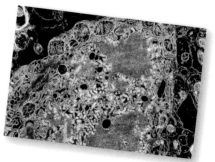

A photograph of the tiny but deadly rabies virus seen under a special microscope. The virus attaches to a healthy nerve cell, then multiplies so that it can infect further cells. With no treatment, it reaches the brain and usually causes death.

When injected into an animal's body, the weaker version of the virus didn't cause a full outbreak of rabies. In fact, it did quite the opposite – it made the body produce substances called antibodies that fought the disease!

For the same reason, young Joseph Meister's treatment proved a huge success. He survived and returned home. Pasteur was acclaimed and patients flocked to Paris. From October 1885 to December 1886, Pasteur and his colleagues treated 2,682 people believed to be infected with rabies. Over 98% of these patients survived. Joseph grew up to be a healthy adult. After serving in the French army during World War I, he worked as a gatekeeper at the Pasteur Institute, by this time a world-leading research center for microbiology and diseases. In 1936, one of the rooms in the institute became a museum of Pasteur's life and work.

The adult Joseph Meister stands next to a statue of Louis Pasteur in 1935. Today, the Pasteur Institute where Meister worked has grown into an international organization with 24 centers around the world.

1877	1879	1884	1885	1886	1888
Starts investigating the deadly disease, anthrax, which strikes humans and animals.	Develops the first ever laboratory vaccine to treat the disease chicken cholera.	Successfully vaccinates dogs with the anti-rabies vaccine for the first time.	Joseph Meister becomes the first person treated for rabies at Pasteur's laboratory.	Nineteen Russians bitten by a rabid wolf visit Pasteur and are given the anti-rabies vaccine successfully.	The Pasteur Institute opens and begins vital research into fighting diseases.

DISCOVERING PENICILLIN

SCIENTIFIC AIMS	▶▶ To treat infected wounds and save lives, especially those of injured soldiers.
CHALLENGES /////////////////////// Not trained as a chemist; didn't have today's high-tech scientific equipment	**WHO ALEXANDER FLEMING** with Howard Florey and Ernst Chain **WHERE** Saint Mary's Hospital, London **WHEN** 1927 to 1940 **METHOD** Fleming was open-minded, curious and observant. He said, 'one sometimes finds what one is not looking for'. He discovered the infection-destroying drug penicillin by accident.
RESULTS	In an experiment, Fleming noticed that a common mold, the same as the mold found on old bread, killed bacteria, or germs. He used this mold, called penicillin, to treat infections.

LIFETIME ACHIEVEMENTS

No. 1

Discovered penicillin, which is a medicine called an antibiotic. Penicillin helped save millions of lives.

No. 2

Discovered that snot contained lysozyme, which is also an antibiotic, but it is not as strong as penicillin.

NAME: Alexander Fleming
BORN: August 6th, 1881
DIED: age 73
NATIONALITY: British
JOB: medical doctor
FAMOUS FOR: discovering penicillin, a medicine that destroys bacteria

→ In 1951, Fleming examines a Petri dish containing a colony, or group, of bacteria. These are the grey streaks. The dish contains a gel that bacteria like to eat. Fleming discovered that penicillin destroyed bacteria in a Petri dish like this.

DISCOVERING PENICILLIN

▶▶ How would Fleming use mold to cure infection?

↑ Penicillin mold is common and can be quite yummy too. It is the kind of mold that grows on Roquefort cheese. It also grows on bread that is left in a damp place for a long time.

↑ It took a long time – until 1945 – for penicillin to be produced in large quantities. All of the jars in this photograph were made in one day but each jar was enough for only one dose.

As usual, the first thing Alexander Fleming did when he entered his laboratory was to check on his latest experiment. He was studying the microscopic germs called bacteria that cause many human illnesses. To his irritation, he saw that a sample was going moldy. Luckily though, the greenish patch of mold appeared on only one of the small glass Petri dishes. The rest were fine.

Off-white patches showed that the bacteria were multiplying steadily. He picked up the moldy dish to rinse it clean. Then he paused, alerted by something strange. All around the green mold, the off-white area had faded – the bacteria here were dead! Something in the mold had killed them.

↑ Fleming in his lab, Petri dish in hand. On the bench is the microscope he used to examine microbes. The inset image shows *penicillium* mold.

PERFECTING PENICILLIN
It took several scientists many years to make penicillin work in small doses. They also discovered how to make the drug on a large scale.

1928 September	1930 November	1938	1941 March
Fleming discovers penicillin.	A baby is treated for an eye infection with penicillin. First cure!	Florey and Chain begin to develop penicillin-based medicines.	After an initial recovery from infection a human subject treated with penicillin dies.

In World War I, Fleming worked in the Royal Army Medical Corps. He witnessed first hand the deadly effects of infections on wounded soldiers.

During World War II, penicillin became extremely valuable. When it was feared that Britain might be invaded, researchers even smeared penicillin on the insides of their coats so that at least some of the medicine would be saved.

Fleming would soon discover that the greenish mold, known as *penicillium notatum*, could kill a range of bacteria. At the time, doctors mainly killed bacteria with chemicals, but often the chemicals did more damage than the bacteria themselves. Fleming had seen a great number of soldiers die of bacterial infections in World War I and he was determined to discover a treatment.

For over a decade, Fleming and his colleagues tried to convert the *penicillium* mold into a usable penicillin medicine. In the end, it was another team made up of Ernst Chain, a chemist, and Howard Florey, a doctor, who succeeded thanks to chemical techniques that Fleming did not know about.
In 1945, all three received a Nobel Prize. But the real winners were the millions of people saved by penicillin, which really deserved its nickname of 'wonder drug'.

Bacteria grow quickly and change into new and different forms. Today, penicillin and other types of antibiotics can no longer destroy many types of bacteria.

1942 March	1943	1944 March	1945 May	1945 June	1957 March
The first life is saved by penicillin.	A moldy melon found in a market in Illinois, USA, is found to contain the world's best penicillin.	Mass production of penicillin begins.	Chemical structure of penicillin is discovered.	Fleming, Florey and Chain receive Nobel Prize in Medicine.	Penicillin made directly from chemicals, rather than from mold, for the first time.

THE FIGHT AGAINST
DISEASE

SCIENTIFIC AIMS	▶▶ To find a cure for diseases. Cancer was her first target. She aimed to cure diseases that could not be treated.
CHALLENGES /////////////////////////////// Found it hard to get a good education and a job in science because she was a woman	**WHO** GERTRUDE ELION **WHERE** Burroughs-Wellcome Company, New York **WHEN** 1944 to 1983 **METHOD** Germs 'feed' on particular chemicals. Elion identified these chemicals and made slightly different versions. When the germs 'fed' on Elion's versions, the changes caused them to die.
RESULTS	Helped find treatments for infections as well as the diseases leukaemia, malaria and gout. Elion found a way to make operations where a healthy organ is put into a new body more successful.

LIFETIME ACHIEVEMENTS

No. 1
Helped develop drugs to make organ transplants far more successful.

No. 2
Found a treatment for leukaemia, a form of cancer.

No. 3
Helped invent acyclovir, the first medicine to work against a range of viruses.

NAME: Gertrude Belle Elion
BORN: January 23rd, 1918
DIED: age 81
NATIONALITY: USA
JOB: medical researcher
FAMOUS FOR: developing a wide range of drugs to treat serious illnesses

→ Gertrude Elion at work in her laboratory in the 1950s. She is wearing a white lab coat to protect against spills.

THE FIGHT AGAINST DISEASE

▶▶ Elion's drug failed to save the last two patients. Would it ever work?

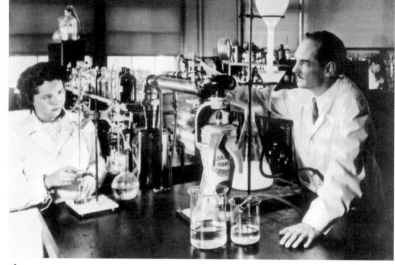

↑ Elion and Hitchings in 1948. Together they worked out a new, less hit-and-miss approach to medical research.

↑ Malaria, a deadly disease spread by mosquitoes, affects millions of people every year. In 1952, Elion helped develop pyrimethamine, the first effective treatment against the disease.

When the phone rang, Trudie Elion hardly dared pick it up. She knew it would be Dr. Joseph Murray. Just a few days before, he had transplanted a kidney into a patient who had been treated with Imuran, the drug she had created. Two years ago, in a dog called Lollipop, the Imuran had worked. It had switched off the body's natural reaction to reject the kidney, and Lollipop had survived.

But last year the drug had failed to protect two human patients because the correct dosage could only be guessed at. Elion wondered what had happened this time: triumph or tragedy? She snatched up the phone, listened intently and smiled. It was good news.

↑ In 1961, Elion and Hitchings invented Imuran. It stopped the bodies of transplant patients from rejecting their new organs and enormously increased survival rates.

ELION TIMELINE	1933	1937	1938	1941
The first part of Elion's life was very tough. As a result of personal tragedies, she decided to devote herself to medical research. Once she overcame prejudice, she went on to triumph against a number of diseases.	Grandfather dies painfully of stomach cancer. Elion devotes herself to medicine.	Applies to 15 graduate schools but is rejected by all of them.	Starts work as a lowly and unpaid volunteer in a chemistry lab.	Leonard Canter, Elion's fiancé, dies of a bacterial infection.

Elion's story is one of patience and determination. She applied to 15 graduate schools, but received unfair treatment because she was a woman. She was rejected by every school. When she finally did get a suitable research job, alongside 73 men and just 1 other woman, the work often consisted of long, repetitive experiments that usually ended in failure. But her determination and her keen intelligence never let her down. Finally, her research was successful – incredibly successful.

Sometimes working with her colleague George Hitchings, sometimes alone, Elion developed drug after drug that saved millions of lives. Sometimes the work was heartbreaking. One of the first drugs she invented was good at treating children with a form of bone cancer called leukaemia – but only for a while. To begin with, every child improved, but then died. It took years to make the drug work properly, but she did it.

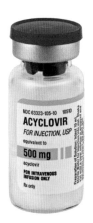

↑ In 1967, Elion's team developed acyclovir, the first anti-viral drug to work against a range of diseases, including herpes, cold sores and glandular fever. She called it her 'final jewel'.

↑ Hitchings and Elion posing for the camera just after receiving the Nobel Prize for medicine in 1988. On the board behind them is the chemical formula of methotrexate, one of the anti-cancer drugs they developed.

↑ Gertrude Elion with her Harvard Medical School colleagues. Elion is petting Lollipop the dog, who received the first successful kidney transplant.

1942	1944	1950	1959	1970s	1988
Finally finds a job as a food analyst. Elion is given dull tasks.	Employed by George Hitchings at Burroughs-Wellcome Institute.	Helps develop a treatment for leukaemia, a form of cancer.	Imuran is used to transplant a kidney into a dog called Lollipop.	Elion's team develop acyclovir, the first medicine to treat a range of viruses.	Receives Nobel Prize for her work with George Hitchings.

MAPPING THE BODY

SCIENTIFIC AIMS	▶▶ To explain how the heart supplies blood to the human body, and what happens to the blood afterwards.
CHALLENGES //////////////////////////////// Disagreed with thousand-year-old ideas; useful microscopes had not been invented	**WHO** WILLIAM HARVEY **WHERE** Cambridge, England and Rome **WHEN** 1615 to 1628 **METHOD** Cutting up the dead bodies of deer and other animals to see how they worked, and then using mathematical calculations to check his ideas.
RESULTS	Harvey was the first person to describe accurately how the heart pumps blood around the body. He proved that the blood circulates, or passes around the body, many times.

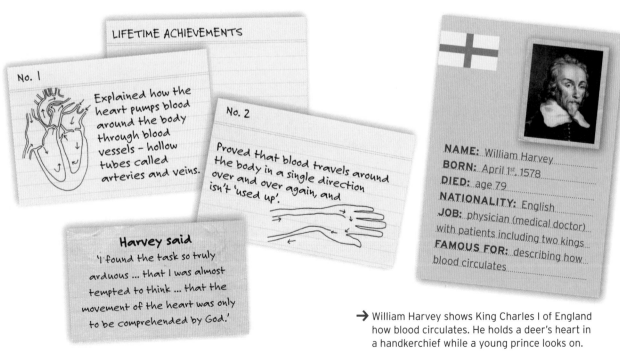

LIFETIME ACHIEVEMENTS

No. 1
Explained how the heart pumps blood around the body through blood vessels – hollow tubes called arteries and veins.

No. 2
Proved that blood travels around the body in a single direction over and over again, and isn't 'used up'.

Harvey said
'I found the task so truly arduous ... that I was almost tempted to think ... that the movement of the heart was only to be comprehended by God.'

NAME: William Harvey
BORN: April 1st 1578
DIED: age 79
NATIONALITY: English
JOB: physician (medical doctor) with patients including two kings
FAMOUS FOR: describing how blood circulates

→ William Harvey shows King Charles I of England how blood circulates. He holds a deer's heart in a handkerchief while a young prince looks on.

MAPPING THE BODY

▶▶ Could Harvey understand how the heart worked? And could he prove it?

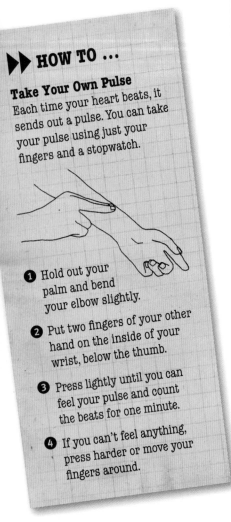

▶▶ HOW TO …

Take Your Own Pulse

Each time your heart beats, it sends out a pulse. You can take your pulse using just your fingers and a stopwatch.

❶ Hold out your palm and bend your elbow slightly.

❷ Put two fingers of your other hand on the inside of your wrist, below the thumb.

❸ Press lightly until you can feel your pulse and count the beats for one minute.

❹ If you can't feel anything, press harder or move your fingers around.

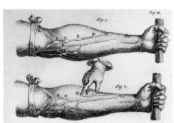

↑ An illustration from Harvey's book *On the Motion of the Heart and Blood*. Harvey found that the bumps in the blood vessels called veins were one-way valves. They made the blood circulate around the body in one direction only.

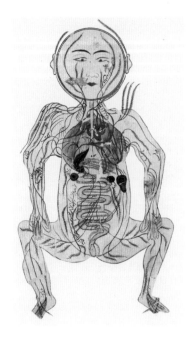

↑ Before Harvey's time, most countries forbade the cutting-up of corpses, so doctors had little idea of how they looked inside. This diagram is typically inaccurate.

Harvey squinted through his magnifying lens at the freshly killed body of the deer. He wanted to prove his theory that blood circulated in the body and was pumped around and around by the heart. But that would mean the tubes called blood vessels that left the heart must be connected with those that returned to it. Could it really be true?

Harvey was convinced that the doctors of his day were wrong. They believed the ancient Greek doctor Galen, who thought that blood was formed in the liver and then used up as soon as it was pumped to the body. The Arab physician Ibn An Nafis and Andreas Vesalius, who, like Harvey, studied at the University of Padua in Italy, both had ideas similar to Harvey's. The question was how to prove them.

The answer lay in Harvey's careful observations and studies. Experimenting on the bodies of animals was gruesome work, but it meant he could be sure that the human heart pumped about two spoonfuls of blood each time it beat. He also knew that it beats about 50,000 times in 24 hours. That meant he could work out just how much blood went through it every day: 2 x 50,000 = 100,000 spoonfuls! Enough blood to fill a huge barrel – there was no way that much could be made and destroyed in a single day. He knew blood must circulate in a system. All Harvey had to do now was to write up his breakthrough in a book. And so he did.

↑ During the English Civil War, Harvey was on the side of King Charles I. He said 'The animal's heart is the basis of its life ... equally is the king the basis of his kingdom's ... from him all power arises and all grace stems.'

As well as being a scientist, Harvey was also a successful doctor, with patients including James I and Charles I, who were both kings of England. His links with the royal court meant he had plenty of freshly killed deer to experiment on. It also gave him the opportunity to travel. He joined a Scottish Duke on a journey around France and Spain at a time when war and plague were raging. There were drawbacks too. In 1642 the first battle of the English Civil War took place, and as physician to the king, Harvey had to be there with him.

Not everyone agreed with Harvey. His theories were so new that some doctors called him 'crack-brained'. Even the great French philosopher Rene Descartes disagreed with him. But Harvey's ground-breaking discoveries about the human body eventually allowed patients to receive successful transfusions of healthy blood. Over time the accuracy of his tests and calculations meant he came to be known as a great experimental physician and a father of modern medical science.

EXTRA

WITCHES & MAGIC

In the 17th century people believed in some superstitions that seem strange to us now.

In 1634, Harvey had to examine four women accused of practicing witchcraft. If they were found guilty, the punishment was hanging. At that time many innocent people were being put to death. Harvey looked at all the evidence and decided that there was a scientific explanation. The 'witches' were found innocent.

Another story claims Harvey once dressed up as a wizard to visit a supposed witch. She had a toad, or 'familiar', which is a magical animal helper. Harvey sent the 'witch' away and cut open the 'familiar', proving that it was nothing more than a common toad. This helped prove that the lady wasn't a witch. It's probably not a true story, but it shows how belief in science gradually overcame superstition.

THE SECRET OF LIFE

SCIENTIFIC AIMS	▶▶ To find the secret of life! DNA, or deoxyribonucleic acid, is like an instruction manual telling your body how to grow.
CHALLENGES //////////////////////////////// A rival scientist on the same mission; modern computers had not yet been invented	**WHO FRANCIS CRICK AND JAMES WATSON** **WHERE** Cambridge University, England **WHEN** 1951 to 1953 **METHOD** They studied X-rays images of DNA and worked out lots of possible DNA shapes. Then they worked out which DNA shape explained the fuzzy images on their X-rays best.
RESULTS	Crick and Watson found out how DNA tells a body to grow and how it allows people to pass on characteristics, such as appearance and behavior, to their children.

NAME: Francis Crick
BORN: June 8th, 1916
DIED: age 88
NATIONALITY: British
JOB: research scientist, professor
FAMOUS FOR: puzzling out the structure of DNA

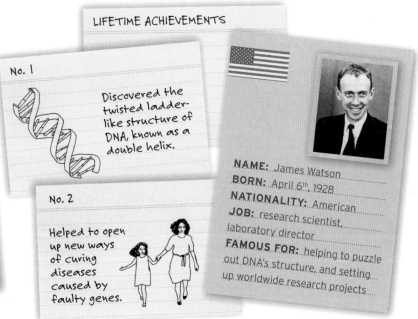

LIFETIME ACHIEVEMENTS

No. 1
Discovered the twisted ladder-like structure of DNA, known as a double helix.

No. 2
Helped to open up new ways of curing diseases caused by faulty genes.

NAME: James Watson
BORN: April 6th, 1928
NATIONALITY: American
JOB: research scientist, laboratory director
FAMOUS FOR: helping to puzzle out DNA's structure, and setting up worldwide research projects

→ Watson (seated) and Crick show the structure of a DNA molecule using a model. Crick points at a 'corner', which represents an atom. A real DNA molecule contains millions of atoms.

THE SECRET OF LIFE

▶▶ Had Crick and Watson really discovered the structure of DNA?

It was lunchtime, on Saturday February 28th, 1953, at the Eagle Pub in Cambridge. As usual, regulars mixed with tourists enjoying food and drink. Suddenly, on the stroke of one o'clock, the door burst open and two excited young men rushed in. Making their way to the bar, they called loudly for drinks. 'This is a celebration,' announced the taller of the pair. 'We've just discovered the secret of life!'

In an incredible piece of scientific detective work, Francis Crick and James Watson had puzzled out the structure of deoxyribonucleic acid, better known by the initials DNA. They were helped in this task by their colleagues Rosalind Franklin and Maurice Wilkins. DNA is found in the billions of cells that make up our bodies. It is the chemical that contains all the instructions that tell our bodies how to grow.

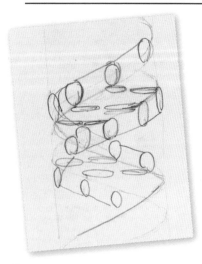

↑ This sketch of the DNA double helix molecule was drawn by Francis Crick in his notebook. Between 1951 and 1953, Crick kept detailed notes on the project.

Wilkins   Crick   Watson

↑ In 1962, Crick and Watson won the Nobel Prize for their work on DNA along with colleague Maurice Wilkins. Since her death, Rosalind Franklin has also been recognized for her important role in the discovery.

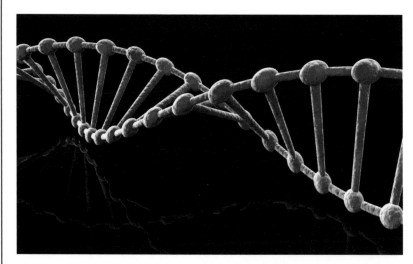

↑ This illustration shows the shape of part of a DNA molecule. The rungs of the ladder, which carry instructions for development and growth, are easy to see.

The DNA race
When Crick and Watson found the structure of DNA, they won a race against a rival scientist called Linus Pauling. Just weeks before they announced their thrilling success, Pauling mistakenly claimed victory.

1951 September	1951 November	1952 May	1953 January
Crick and Watson begin work in the UK. Linus Pauling starts on the same mission in the US.	Rosalind Franklin gives a talk about her X-ray scans of DNA. Watson is in the audience.	Franklin takes an X-ray photo of DNA clearer than anything seen before, but does not release it.	Pauling sends a paper with his idea of the structure of DNA to his son in London.

A DNA molecule looks like a twisted ladder, but the rungs of DNA are not all the same. They are a bit like the different letters in an alphabet. They can be arranged to form instructions, just like letters can be arranged to make sentences. Each instruction is called a gene. One gene might be 'the eye color is blue.' Another might be 'the hair is brown.' The genes on every person's DNA are slightly different, except for those of identical twins.

↑ Today, it is possible to change the structure of an animal's DNA to produce a new creature, like this glow-in-the-dark mouse!

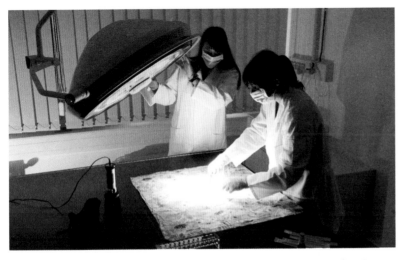

↑ Two lab technicians examine criminal evidence for possible traces of DNA under an ultraviolet light.

James Watson said
'Imagination comes first in both scientific and artistic creations, but in science there is only one answer and that has to be correct.'

↑ A scientist inspects DNA samples collected for the Human Genome Project. This scientific study took over ten years to order and identify the billions of chemical units in human DNA.

Thanks to the discoveries of Crick and Watson, and other scientists, we can now treat a vast range of illnesses caused by faulty genes. We can also track down criminals from tiny traces of DNA in their blood. Their work has also led to the Human Genome Project, which studies the exact pattern of genes in people. It has revealed which parts of the DNA molecule control which characteristics in a person.

1953 January	1953 January	1953 February	1953 February	1953 March	1953 April
Watson reads the paper and realizes Pauling is close to making a discovery.	Franklin's colleague gives Watson the clear X-ray photo without her permission.	Pauling publishes his paper, but Crick, Watson and Franklin think that Pauling's DNA structure is wrong.	Crick and Watson are sure their model is correct. They announce it in the pub.	Crick and Watson finish making their model.	They publish an essay in the journal *Nature*, and win the DNA race!

LAWS OF THE UNIVERSE

SCIENTIFIC AIMS	▶▶ To write down scientific laws about how everything in the universe moves and how everything is connected.
CHALLENGES /// Computers had not yet been invented; searched the Bible looking for scientific answers	**WHO ISAAC NEWTON** **WHERE** Lincolnshire and Cambridge, England **WHEN** 1663 to 1713 **METHOD** Came up with new theories of movement and gravity and checked whether he was correct by using a new kind of mathematics that he had invented.
RESULTS	Newton explained how the planets move and why the moon orbits, or goes around, the Earth. He discovered the law of gravity, which is a force that holds you on the Earth.

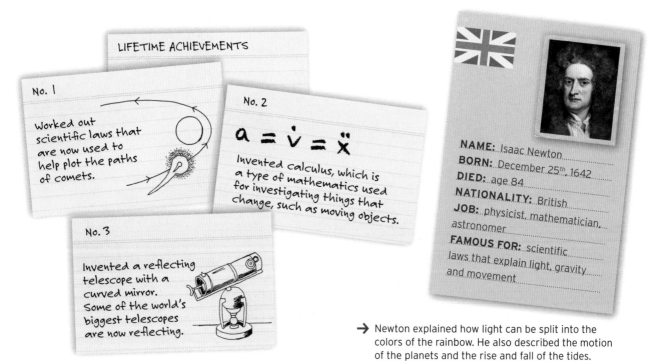

LIFETIME ACHIEVEMENTS

No. 1
Worked out scientific laws that are now used to help plot the paths of comets.

No. 2
$$a = \dot{v} = \ddot{x}$$
Invented calculus, which is a type of mathematics used for investigating things that change, such as moving objects.

No. 3
Invented a reflecting telescope with a curved mirror. Some of the world's biggest telescopes are now reflecting.

NAME: Isaac Newton
BORN: December 25th, 1642
DIED: age 84
NATIONALITY: British
JOB: physicist, mathematician, astronomer
FAMOUS FOR: scientific laws that explain light, gravity and movement

→ Newton explained how light can be split into the colors of the rainbow. He also described the motion of the planets and the rise and fall of the tides.

LAWS OF THE UNIVERSE

▶▶ Simple laws could explain the universe, if Newton could find them ...

↑ Newton was born in this farmhouse on Christmas Eve 1642. His mother hoped he would be a farmer, but he wasn't very good at farming.

↑ This portrait of Newton, age 46, was painted two years after the publication of his most important discoveries. It shows Newton with his own hair, rather than a wig, which was unusual for a portrait of the day.

Newton said
'I do not know what I may appear to the world, but to myself I seem to have been only like a boy playing on the sea shore ...'

In 1665, many of England's greatest cities faced disaster. Thousands of people died from a disease known as the Black Death, and those who survived fled the cities in fear. Isaac Newton was one of the lucky ones. He rushed to his family farm in the small village of Woolsthorpe in Lincolnshire. Here he made one of the greatest scientific discoveries of all.

↑ One of the most famous stories about Newton is that a falling apple made him understand the law of gravity.

Newton realized that the Moon orbits, or goes round, the Earth for the same reason that falling objects, including apples, are pulled to the ground. The force of gravity causes both of these things. He became determined to find out how gravity works.

Newton defined three laws of motion. The first says that a moving object continues in the same direction and speed unless forces act upon it. Think about kicking a ball. The force of gravity pulls it to the ground and air slows it down. The second law explains that the harder the force, the faster the speed. So, the harder you kick a ball, the further it goes. The third law says that if an object is pulled or pushed, it pulls or pushes back. So, your foot is a force on the ball. But the ball puts the same amount of force on your foot – you feel it when you kick.

Next, Newton defined the law of universal gravitation. Newton understood that the same laws of science apply everywhere in the universe. There is a gravitational force between you and Earth. There is also a gravitational force between you and the Sun. But you fall toward Earth, rather than toward the Sun because the force between you and the Earth is stronger.

Newton put all his laws to use. He wrote them down as mathematical sums and then applied them to his studies of the Moon and the planets. He predicted, or figured out, how the planets and the Moon would move. As Newton put it, he'd discovered, 'the frame of the system of the world'.

1. Earth's gravity pulls on the falling apple.

2. Gravity also pulls on the Moon, but the Moon is on the move.

4. The Moon doesn't fall to Earth.

3. So the Moon orbits instead.

↑ Newton uses a prism to split white light into colors. He liked sevens, so he decided there were seven colors, although the seventh, indigo, was really a shade of blue.

↑ The law of gravity tells us that there is a force pulling objects to Earth. That same force keeps the Moon in its orbit. Newton's third law states that the Moon and other objects pull back on the Earth just as hard.

↑ An unlikely tale about Newton is that his dog set fire to his work by knocking over a candle. It is said that he cut a hole in his door for the dog to climb through and a smaller one for her puppies.

Newton studied other aspects of science too, including light. He discovered that white light could be split up into a rainbow of colors by a shaped piece of glass called a prism. He realized that those same colors could be mixed to make white light again.

LAWS OF THE UNIVERSE

▶▶ Simple laws could explain the universe, if Newton could find them ...

▶▶ HOW TO ...

Make a Rainbow

Newton split sunlight into a rainbow of colors. He called it a spectrum. Real rainbows use raindrops to split the light. Newton used a piece of glass called a prism, but you can use an old CD.

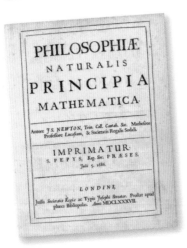

❶ Wait for a sunny day.

❷ Take a CD and wipe it clean.

❸ Put it label-down on a sunlit window sill.

❹ Look at the CD and you should see a rainbow on its surface.

PHILOSOPHIÆ
NATURALIS
PRINCIPIA
MATHEMATICA.

Autore JS. NEWTON, Trin. Coll. Cantab. Soc. Mathescos Professore Lucasiano, & Societatis Regalis Sodali.

IMPRIMATUR.
S. PEPYS, Reg. Soc. PRÆSES.
Julii 5. 1686.

LONDINI,
Jussu Societatis Regiæ ac Typis Josephi Streater. Prostat apud plures Bibliopolas. Anno MDCLXXXVII.

↑ This book by Isaac Newton is one of the most important books ever written. The title is in Latin and reads *Mathematical Principles of Natural Philosophy*.

As a child, Newton loved building scientific toys. He also learnt the secrets of medicine from a local apothecary. This was a person who gave out medicine, like a pharmacist does today. When Newton was 19, he joined Cambridge University, where he remained for most of his life. Here he studied the mysteries of light, motion and mathematics, but he told only a few people of his discoveries.

Then, in 1684, Edmond Halley, a fellow mathematician and astronomer, came to ask Newton for help. Halley and his colleagues were trying – and failing – to work out the mathematical formula to describe the orbits of the planets. Long ago, Newton had worked out the answer for himself. Halley was so impressed that he paid for the publication of Newton's work, the *Principia*. This book explained the laws of motion and showed how they could be used to work out the movements of any objects on which forces, including gravity, act. Newton used a new type of math called calculus to figure out the answers but he kept this secret by explaining them through geometry, which is clumsier and more long-winded.

↑ This statue is based on a painting of Newton made by a poet and artist called William Blake. It shows Newton unlocking the secrets of the world.

↑ Newton was a skilled craftsman. He not only built this telescope but also the tools he needed to construct it.

From then on, Newton was famous. He joined the Royal Society, which was England's main scientific group, and later became its president. In 1704, he published his discoveries about light in a second major book, *The Opticks*. He even received a knighthood from Queen Anne. This was a rare honor for a scientist. Only one scientist, Francis Bacon, had received a knighthood before, over a century earlier.

Newton was also put in charge of the Royal Mint, where England's money was made. He was given this well-paid job as a reward for his discoveries and was not expected to do much. However, at this time, many people clipped the edges of coins to keep some of their valuable metal. This meant many coins weighed less than half of what they should. Often, the metal was used to make fake coins by criminals called coiners. Newton worked hard to remedy this situation, even disguising himself as a coiner to entrap the criminals!

EXPERIMENTS IN
SPACE AND TIME

SCIENTIFIC AIMS	▶▶ To answer some of the biggest questions of all: what are time, space and gravity?

CHALLENGES	**WHO** ALBERT EINSTEIN
////////////////////////////	**WHERE** Germany, Switzerland and the USA
He needed to learn advanced mathematics; powerful people disagreed with his ideas	**WHEN** 1905 to 1955
	METHOD Einstein developed mathematical models, wrote formulas and made calculations to explore his groundbreaking ideas. He thought about things in new and different ways.

RESULTS	Einstein changed the way scientists thought about time, space and gravity. Thanks to him, we can now understand how the universe formed and developed.

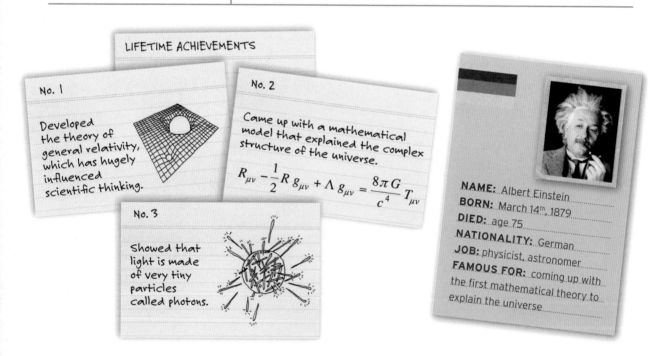

LIFETIME ACHIEVEMENTS

No. 1

Developed the theory of general relativity, which has hugely influenced scientific thinking.

No. 2

Came up with a mathematical model that explained the complex structure of the universe.

$$R_{\mu\nu} - \frac{1}{2} R\, g_{\mu\nu} + \Lambda\, g_{\mu\nu} = \frac{8\pi G}{c^4} T_{\mu\nu}$$

No. 3

Showed that light is made of very tiny particles called photons.

NAME: Albert Einstein
BORN: March 14th, 1879
DIED: age 75
NATIONALITY: German
JOB: physicist, astronomer
FAMOUS FOR: coming up with the first mathematical theory to explain the universe

→ Einstein's triumph was his theory of general relativity: the discovery that massive objects such as planets cause a distortion, felt as gravity, that affects space and time in the universe. Huge masses can even bend light.

▶▶ Could Einstein's theory of relativity really explain the universe?

↑ Einstein did his early scientific work while he had a job as a clerk in an office. Later he worked in a university. This picture shows him sitting at his office desk.

▶▶ HOW TO ...

Travel in Time
One day, Einstein's ideas might make time travel possible. This could be how ...

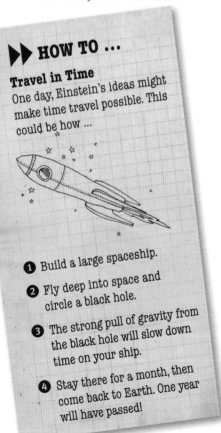

1 Build a large spaceship.

2 Fly deep into space and circle a black hole.

3 The strong pull of gravity from the black hole will slow down time on your ship.

4 Stay there for a month, then come back to Earth. One year will have passed!

↑ This photo, taken on May 29th, 1919, shows a total solar eclipse. This occurs when the Moon passes between the Sun and Earth, completely blocking out the Sun.

The meeting room at the Royal Society was full of chatter, but silence fell when the speaker stood to announce the results that everyone had gathered to hear. He cleared his throat, shuffled his papers and began: 'The eclipse measurements have now been fully studied, and the result is clear. The stars close to the Sun did indeed move closer together as the Sun passed by, just as general relativity predicts.' Albert Einstein was not there to hear the words because he was certain that his theory was true. Now the world had proof. Over the next few days, the newspapers trumpeted Einstein's triumph.

In 1919, the British scientist Arthur Eddington had headed a long and risky expedition to the island of Príncipe, off the west coast of Africa, to view a total eclipse of the Sun. From the island, Eddington could take photos of the dark daytime sky during the eclipse and test out Einstein's theory. Only under these conditions was it possible to see stars in the part of the sky close to the Sun.

If Einstein was right, the enormous gravity, or 'pull', of the Sun would disturb the space and time around it. Starlight passing through the disturbed area would bend and make the stars seem to move. The photos that Eddington took of the starlit sky showed exactly that.

Imagine time speeding up! Einstein's relativity theory totally changed our understanding of the universe and time. People thought that time ticked on at one speed, but Einstein showed that time could speed up or slow down as speed and gravity came into play. Also, Einstein made another big discovery. Scientists had thought of light as a wave traveling through space, like ripples on a pond, but Einstein discovered that light is made up of tiny 'packets' of energy called photons.

One of Einstein's most famous discoveries is the equation $E = mc^2$. The idea is complicated but basically it means that energy (E) and mass (m) – the measure of the amount of 'stuff' in an object – are equal to one another. Einstein showed that mass could appear as energy. Today, releasing energy from matter is the basis for nuclear power. Einstein died in 1955 but his ideas about space, time, mass and energy are still used by scientists today.

↑ This sculpture of Einstein's world-famous equation was part of an exhibition called the Walk of Ideas in Germany, the country where Einstein was born.

INVESTIGATING RADIOACTIVITY

## SCIENTIFIC AIMS	▶▶ To investigate powerful invisible rays, known as gamma rays, found in the metal uranium.
## CHALLENGES ////////////////////////////// Working in dangerous conditions; risk of illness; long exhausting hours	**WHO** **MARIE CURIE** along with her husband Pierre Curie **WHERE** Paris, France **WHEN** 1897 to 1910 **METHOD** Examined a mineral called pitchblende, which contained uranium but gave off more gamma rays than uranium by itself. She studied the ingredients in the pitchblende.
## RESULTS	Curie discovered two new chemical elements, which she named radium and polonium. She used them to make new medical treatments. They gave off particles and energy waves, which she called radioactivity.

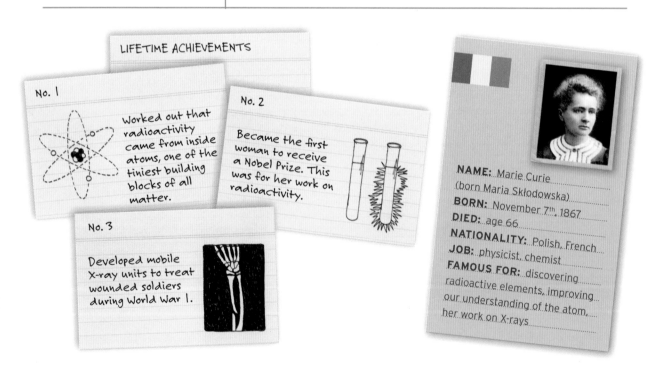

LIFETIME ACHIEVEMENTS

No. 1 — Worked out that radioactivity came from inside atoms, one of the tiniest building blocks of all matter.

No. 2 — Became the first woman to receive a Nobel Prize. This was for her work on radioactivity.

No. 3 — Developed mobile X-ray units to treat wounded soldiers during World War 1.

NAME: Marie Curie (born Maria Skłodowska)
BORN: November 7th, 1867
DIED: age 66
NATIONALITY: Polish, French
JOB: physicist, chemist
FAMOUS FOR: discovering radioactive elements, improving our understanding of the atom, her work on X-rays

→ Marie Curie examines a sample in her laboratory. Her pioneering work led to many developments in physics and medicine, including treatments for cancer.

▶▶ Could Marie Curie unlock the secrets of radium before it destroyed her?

One winter's evening in 1903, Marie Curie and her husband Pierre made their way to the crumbling old building that served as their laboratory. Night was falling fast and it was already so dark that Marie had to fumble with the key before they could get in.

When the door finally swung back, both scientists stopped in amazement. Instead of the gloomy interior they were expecting, test tubes and jars lit up the room with a soft green glow. It was the glow from a new chemical element, called radium, and they were the first people ever to see it.

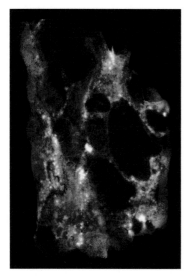

↑ This is a sample of radium. The atoms that make up the element are unstable. They break down to release energy in the form of gamma rays and other kinds of radiation.

Marie Curie said
'Never let oneself be beaten down by persons or by events.'

↑ Curie had no interest in clothes. She even asked for a wedding dress that would also be suitable for lab work. This is the only hat she is ever known to have bought, for a trip to the USA to raise research funds.

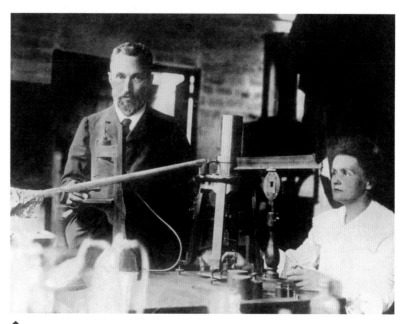

↑ Many photos of the Curies show Marie sitting down while Pierre stands. In reality, Marie did most of the heavy physical work involved in extracting radium.

In 1896, scientist Henri Becquerel discovered that the metal uranium gave off radioactivity. Gamma rays are the most powerful kind of radioactivity. These waves of energy can pass through the human body with ease. What Becquerel didn't realize at the time was that gamma rays inflict devastating damage. Large doses cause radiation sickness that can kill within days, and even small amounts can trigger cancers that may take years to appear.

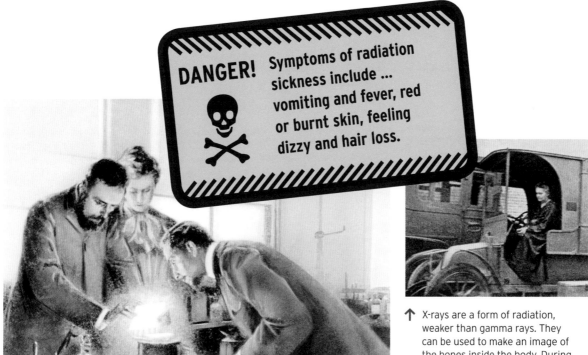

↑ Pierre and Marie Curie show their discovery to a fellow scientist. Pierre is using his bare hands because the deadly nature of radium was unknown at the time.

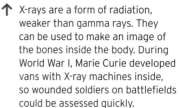

↑ X-rays are a form of radiation, weaker than gamma rays. They can be used to make an image of the bones inside the body. During World War I, Marie Curie developed vans with X-ray machines inside, so wounded soldiers on battlefields could be assessed quickly.

Following in Becquerel's footsteps, the Curies started to study pitchblende, which contained uranium. They discovered it gave off *more* gamma rays than uranium alone – there had to be something else in the pitchblende causing this to happen. After years of painstaking work, the Curies separated the various elements in pitchblende and found the new elements polonium and radium. When Pierre was killed in a traffic accident in 1906, Marie worked on alone. She died in 1934 at the age of 66, after years of being exposed to highly dangerous radioactivity.

In 1903 and 1911, Marie Curie was awarded the Nobel Prize, first for her work in physics and then in chemistry. She also set up medical institutes in France and Poland. At these places and elsewhere, doctors learned to treat cancers with radium. Today the use of radioactive materials is vital to medicine. The Curies' research also helped to found the science of nuclear physics, which looks at how atoms work.

THE GREAT RADIUM DANCE

THE RADIUM DANCE

by JEAN SCHWARTZ

As Introduced in "PIFF·PAFF·POUF"

↑ Radium caught the imagination of the public in a big and strange way. People assumed – for no good reason – that it could cure almost anything. It even had a dance named after it! At least one group of dancers from Paris wore glowing veils.

THE PERIODIC TABLE

## SCIENTIFIC AIMS	▶▶ To sort and group together the building blocks of chemistry – these are called elements.
## CHALLENGES /////////////////////////////////////// Some pieces of this scientific puzzle were missing; other scientists were hot on his tail	**WHO** DMITRI MENDELEEV **WHERE** St. Petersburg, Russia **WHEN** 1865 to 1869 **METHOD** An element is a substance, such as gold or iron, that cannot be broken down into simpler substances. Mendeleev figured out how the elements could be gathered together into similar sets.
## RESULTS	He worked out a table based on how the elements behaved and a scientific measurement called atomic weight. His findings showed him that new elements were still to be discovered.

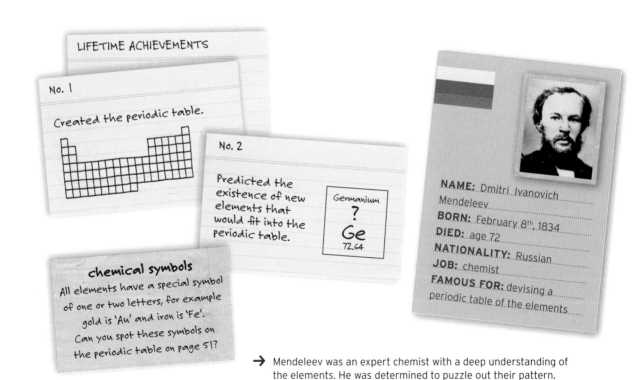

LIFETIME ACHIEVEMENTS

No. 1

Created the periodic table.

No. 2

Predicted the existence of new elements that would fit into the periodic table.

Germanium
?
Ge
72.64

chemical symbols
All elements have a special symbol of one or two letters, for example gold is 'Au' and iron is 'Fe'. Can you spot these symbols on the periodic table on page 51?

NAME: Dmitri Ivanovich Mendeleev
BORN: February 8th, 1834
DIED: age 72
NATIONALITY: Russian
JOB: chemist
FAMOUS FOR: devising a periodic table of the elements

→ Mendeleev was an expert chemist with a deep understanding of the elements. He was determined to puzzle out their pattern.

THE PERIODIC TABLE

▶▶ Was Mendeleev's hunch that there were new elements correct?

↑ Mendeleev was in his 30s when he worked out the patterns in his periodic table.

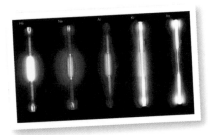

↑ In 1902, a few years before he died, Mendeleev added the noble gases to his table. These include helium, neon and argon. They glow when electricity is passed through them.

Mendelevium
101
Md
[258]

↑ In 1955, a new element was added to the periodic table. It was given the name mendelevium in honor of Mendeleev and his work.

Dmitri Mendeleev glared at the pieces of card on the table. On each of them, he had written the name of an element and a special scientific measurement named called 'atomic weight'. Hydrogen is roughly 1, calcium 40, iron 56, gold 197 and so on. There was a pattern here somewhere, he was sure of it. Once again, he arranged the cards in order of their atomic weight, and in rows of different lengths.

Sure enough, the elements at the beginning of the rows were similar to each other, and so were the elements at the end. But in between it was a mess. It looked like a card game that hadn't worked out! If he didn't find a pattern soon, he felt sure a rival chemist would beat him to it.

Mendeleev pushed at the cards, making gaps in the pattern, then he paused. Could that be the answer? The gaps in the table? Suddenly, the truth struck him – the gaps weren't in the sequence of the elements, they were gaps in human knowledge. There must be elements that scientists hadn't discovered yet! These elements would fit into the gaps.

Excitedly, he arranged the cards again, but this time he left the gaps in the rows so that he could keep similar elements together. It worked. At last he had a table in which each column contained similar elements.

↑ This is the element gold. It is unusual because it is found in a pure form. Most elements are found joined to other elements, for example, uranium is part of the ore pitchblende. This is one of the reasons it was tricky to find new elements.

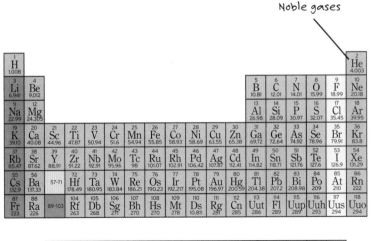

Noble gases

1 H 1.008																	2 He 4.003
3 Li 6.941	4 Be 9.012											5 B 10.81	6 C 12.01	7 N 14.01	8 O 15.99	9 F 18.99	10 Ne 20.18
11 Na 22.99	12 Mg 24.305											13 Al 26.98	14 Si 28.09	15 P 30.97	16 S 32.07	17 Cl 35.45	18 Ar 39.95
19 K 39.10	20 Ca 40.08	21 Sc 44.96	22 Ti 47.87	23 V 50.94	24 Cr 51.6	25 Mn 54.94	26 Fe 55.85	27 Co 58.93	28 Ni 58.69	29 Cu 63.55	30 Zn 65.38	31 Ga 69.72	32 Ge 72.64	33 As 74.92	34 Se 78.96	35 Br 79.91	36 Kr 83.8
37 Rb 85.47	38 Sr 87.62	39 Y 88.91	40 Zr 91.22	41 Nb 92.91	42 Mo 95.96	43 Tc 98	44 Ru 101.07	45 Rh 102.91	46 Pd 106.42	47 Ag 107.87	48 Cd 112.41	49 In 114.82	50 Sn 118.71	51 Sb 121.76	52 Te 127.6	53 I 126.9	54 Xe 131.29
55 Cs 132.9	56 Ba 137.33	57–71	72 Hf 178.49	73 Ta 180.95	74 W 183.84	75 Re 186.21	76 Os 190.23	77 Ir 192.217	78 Pt 195.08	79 Au 196.97	80 Hg 200.59	81 Tl 204.38	82 Pb 207.2	83 Bi 208.98	84 Po 209	85 At 210	86 Rn 222
87 Fr 223	88 Ra 226	89–103	104 Rf 263	105 Db 268	106 Sg 271	107 Bh 270	108 Hs 270	109 Mt 278	110 Ds 10.811	111 Rg 281	112 Cn 285	113 Uut 286	114 Fl 289	115 Uup 289	116 Uuh 293	117 Uus 294	118 Uuo 294

57 La 138.9	58 Ce 140.12	59 Pr 140.9	60 Nd 144.24	61 Pm 145	62 Sm 150.36	63 Eu 151.96	64 Gd 157.25	65 Tb 158.93	66 Dy 162.5	67 Ho 164.93	68 Er 167.26	69 Tm 168.93	70 Yb 173.05	71 Lu 174.96
89 Ac 227	90 Th 232.04	91 Pa 231.04	92 U 238.03	93 Np 237	94 Pu 244	95 Am 243	96 Cm 247	97 Bk 247	98 Cf 251	99 Es 252	100 Fm 257	101 Md 258	102 No 259	103 Lr 262

↑ This is a modern-day periodic table. Similar elements, such as the noble gases, are grouped together in vertical columns. The rows are known as periods. In the rows, elements are arranged in order of their increasing atomic number.

Mendeleev now realized something else. Since he knew where each gap was, he could work out things about the undiscovered elements that would one day fill those gaps. He had a rough idea that an element's atomic weight was between the weights of the elements on either side. He also knew that its properties, such as whether it was a gas or a solid at room temperature, must be similar to the elements above and below it in the column.

In 1869, Mendeleev published his periodic table together with descriptions of the properties of elements that he believed would one day be found. Ten years later, a new element called scandium was discovered. Sure enough, its properties were similar to those that Mendeleev had worked out.

Within a few decades, scientists had found all the missing elements, and their properties matched Mendeleev's predictions. Mendeleev's periodic table was complete. Today, every chemistry laboratory has a periodic table on the wall. It is only a little different to Mendeleev's table. Among other things, the periodic table can be used to work out how one element will react with another one.

THE POWER OF
ELECTRICITY

SCIENTIFIC AIMS	▶▶ To unlock the secrets of electricity and magnetism. Their hidden powers would transform the world!
CHALLENGES /////////////////////////////// Born in a slum to poor parents; received little education; bad at math	**WHO** MICHAEL FARADAY **WHERE** London, England **WHEN** 1813 to 1831 **METHOD** Came up with a theory, or set of ideas, then tested it by carrying out experiments. If the results did not fit his ideas, Faraday changed the theory and did more experiments.
RESULTS	Faraday came up with the first modern theory that connected electricity to magnetism. He was the first person to produce an electric current by using a magnetic field.

LIFETIME ACHIEVEMENTS

No. 1

Invented the electric motor and the dynamo, which generates electricity.

No. 2

Developed the theory of electromagnetism based on tests that involved magnetic fields.

No. 3

Started a series of popular science lectures, or talks, that are still held once a year.

NAME: Michael Faraday
BORN: September 22nd, 1791
DIED: age 75
NATIONALITY: British
JOB: laboratory assistant
FAMOUS FOR: inventions and discoveries on which most of our modern technology is based

→ Michael Faraday was a great experimental scientist. This photo was taken a few years before he died. The tall object next to him is a Leyden jar, a device that stores electricity.

THE POWER OF ELECTRICITY

▶▶ Could Faraday find the hidden link between electricity and magnetism?

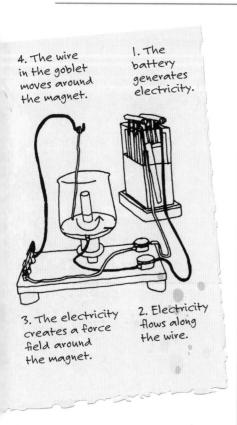

4. The wire in the goblet moves around the magnet.

1. The battery generates electricity.

3. The electricity creates a force field around the magnet.

2. Electricity flows along the wire.

↑ This diagram shows Faraday's electric motor experiment. He transformed electricity into movement using a battery, a magnet and a goblet filled with mercury. Mercury is liquid at room temperature and conducts electricity.

↑ Today, all kinds of machines in our homes, from fridges and washing machines to hair dryers, have electric motors. In the future, all our cars may run on electric motors rather than liquid fuel.

↑ Faraday was a chemist as well as a physicist. Here he is at work in his research laboratory at the Royal Institution in London.

Our modern world, full of power and gadgets, began on Tuesday, September 3rd, 1822. On that day, in a London laboratory, Michael Faraday crouched over his wooden bench, carefully assembling his equipment. Over ten years, he had tried countless times to achieve one of his dreams – to draw on the hidden power of electricity and magnetism. Faraday tried his experiment yet again. He checked that the magnet was fixed in the middle of the goblet filled with mercury. Then he connected a wire from the battery to the mercury in the goblet.

Not expecting a great deal, Faraday connected the end of a second wire to the other pole of the battery. Then he gently dangled the end of this wire into the mercury. Silent and invisible, electricity began to flow from the battery. It traveled down the dangling wire, through the mercury, along the other wire and back to the battery again. The electricity in the dangling wire had generated a magnetic field. The magnet's own force pushed back against it, making the wire move. As the wire swung around, circling the magnet in the goblet, Faraday knew he had proved his theory. He had transformed electricity into movement and invented the electric motor!

DANGER! Faraday was brave in his experiments. He even tested the power from electric eels by holding them in his hands!

Faraday's invention was the first of many that would transform the world and give us electric power. Without it, we would have no computers, telephones, cars, airplanes or modern lights. He could have been an extremely rich man but he had no interest in money. It was the discoveries he made that filled him with excitement.

Faraday made huge developments in many other areas. As well as his discoveries in physics and chemistry, he transformed the way science was taught by making it popular and exciting, especially to young people. In 1825, he started the Royal Institution Christmas Lectures in London. These are yearly talks given on a scientific topic. Faraday also campaigned against pollution and worked tirelessly for his church. When he died in 1867, probably as a result of the dangerous chemicals he had used in his experiments, he had become one of the most famous men in the country.

↑ Faraday gives one of his popular Christmas lectures at the Royal Institution. They still continue today and are shown on television.

EXTRA

ESSENTIAL INVENTIONS

Faraday invented things to help with his research. Many were so useful that we still use them today.

Faraday's dynamo, or generator, turned the movement of a spinning disc into electricity. It is used today in power stations to turn falling water into electricity that powers our homes.

This person is safe from artificial lightning because he is inside a metal cage. The electricity stays on the outside of the cage. It's called a Faraday cage, and is used to protect people and electric equiment.

The next time you blow up a balloon at a birthday party, stop and think. Faraday invented rubber balloons to help him in his experiments!

NAMING THE NATURAL WORLD

SCIENTIFIC AIMS	▶▶ To invent a clear and simple naming system that could be used for every living thing.
CHALLENGES /////////////////////////////// There are over 8 million kinds of living things; he had little money to support himself	**WHO CARL LINNAEUS** **WHERE** Sweden **WHEN** 1730 to 1778 **METHOD** Made trips to Lapland and Norway to study. He grouped living things according to features they shared, such as spines or petals. He gave each living thing a simple two-part scientific name.
RESULTS	Simple scientific names made it easier for scientists to share information. Today, students and scientists still use a system that is much the same as the one created by Linnaeus.

LIFETIME ACHIEVEMENTS

No. 1

Found new kinds of plants and animals and grouped them into a system.

No. 2

Catalogued and grouped over 12,000 animals and plants.

NAME: Carl Linnaeus

BORN: May 23rd 1707

DIED: age 70

NATIONALITY: Swedish

JOB: biologist

FAMOUS FOR: coming up with a method of naming plants and animals that we still use today

→ Here Linnaeus hold a plant called the twinflower and wears the traditional costume of Lapland. He first explored the region, which includes the Arctic area of Finland, in 1732.

NAMING THE
NATURAL WORLD

▶▶ Could Linnaeus really find a simple way to describe every living thing?

↑ Before Linnaeus, the scientific names of plants and animals were often very long and confusing. This common dog rose was called *Rosa sylvestris inodora seu canina*. Linnaeus simplified it to *Rosa canina*.

↑ This strange stuffed creature, called the Hamburg hydra, was said to be real. When Linnaeus saw it in 1735, he spotted at once that it was a fake!

↑ Linnaeus had loyal students who helped him to study wildlife. Joseph Banks and Daniel Solander traveled to Australia with Captain Cook and discovered hundreds of new plants.

↑ Linnaeus's expeditions were difficult and dangerous. Once, he even fell into a deep crevasse. Battered and bruised, he needed two men to rescue him.

Linnaeus and his horse were getting tired. His expedition around Lapland had been exciting and successful. He had discovered all sorts of plants and animals never recorded before. But he was still puzzling over a problem. The best-known animals in the world were the four-legged ones, so he wanted to find a way to organize them into related groups. But there were so many kinds and they were all different from one another – he just couldn't find a way.

As he wondered, Linnaeus noticed a whitish object by the roadside. It was a jawbone. He stopped to look at it. Maybe it was yet another unknown type of animal. But as soon as he picked it up, he recognized that it came from a horse.

Suddenly, Linnaeus realized that he had been able to identify the animal at once. What was it about the jawbone that gave him the answer? It was the teeth! This was also the answer to his bigger puzzle. Along with a few other pieces of information, he could classify different types of four-legged animals by the type and number of teeth that they had.

Today, scientists still use a similar system to Linnaeus, although many of the details are different. There are an enormous number of living things that Linnaeus did not know about, including many that are neither plants nor animals, so our system has to be much larger. Part of the modern system is shown on the right. Like Linnaeus's system, it has several levels. Each kingdom, such as the animal kingdom, contains several large groups called phyla. Each phylum has several classes and so on. The bottom two levels are the genus and the species. These levels are used to name every living thing. So, the brown bear is the species *Ursus arctos*, belonging to the genus *Ursus*.

When Linnaeus had completed his six-month expedition, he lost no time in writing up his findings in a book, called *Plants of Lapland* in English. It was to be the first of many.

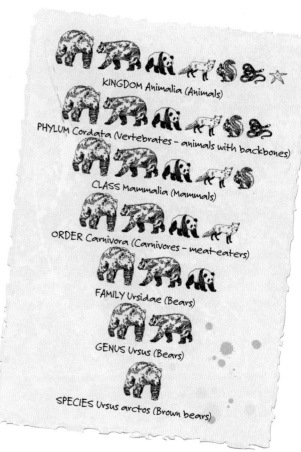

↑ Here you can see how the brown bear is classified and named according to the modern version of Linnaeus's system.

↑ Linnaeus's book about the plants of Lapland was the first to use his two great inventions: a way of naming any living thing using just two Latin words, and his system of showing how different living things are related to each other.

↑ This is the goldsmith beetle, an insect discovered by *Linnaeus*. He gave it the scientific name *Cetonia aurata. Cetonia* is the genus, or group, of beetles that it belongs to. The word *aurata* means 'golden' and describes the species.

THE THEORY OF EVOLUTION

SCIENTIFIC AIMS	▶▶ To show that over many years plants and animals on Earth evolved, or gradually developed, from simpler ones.
CHALLENGES ///////////////////////////////// Many religious people disagreed with his ideas; he was often in poor health	**WHO** **CHARLES DARWIN** **WHERE** all over the world **WHEN** 1831 to 1858 **METHOD** Darwin traveled for thousands of miles on a ship called HMS *Beagle*. The journey lasted over four years. During this time, he collected an enormous amount of information about living things.
RESULTS	Darwin proved that today's plants and animals came about from simpler ones through a long, slow process, stretching over millions of years, called evolution.

LIFETIME ACHIEVEMENTS

No. 1

Discovered some living things were more suited to their surroundings and did well.

No. 2

His ideas about evolution helped to prove that the Earth was extremely old.

NAME: Charles Robert Darwin
BORN: February 12th, 1809
DIED: age 73
NATIONALITY: British
JOB: biologist
FAMOUS FOR: the theory of evolution, which explains how living things change over time, adapting to suit their surroundings

→ A portrait of Charles Darwin as young man in his thirties. Around this time, he was developing his ideas about evolution and gaining a reputation as a brilliant scientist.

THE THEORY OF EVOLUTION

▶▶ How would Darwin prove that living things evolve over millions of years?

↑ The HMS *Beagle* seen in the Strait of Magellan, at the southern tip of South America. The *Beagle* was one of the first boats to be fitted with a lightning conductor, and survived several strikes during the voyage.

▶▶ HOW TO ...

Track Animals in the Wild

Tracking is easy on a flat beach with damp sand, but with skill you can do it anywhere.

❶ Look out for footprints. If they have crisp edges, it means they are fresh.

❷ Keep your eyes peeled for droppings. If they are damp or smelly, they are recent.

❸ Chewed plants oozing sap mean that an animal has passed by recently.

Charles Darwin had been on board the HMS *Beagle* for more than three years when he arrived at the Galapagos Islands. For the crew, the islands were a nightmare. They had to climb over dangerous rocks, the sun beat down and some of the plants smelled disgusting. But for Charles Darwin, it was paradise. Animals he had never seen before crowded the shore, from giant lizards to lumbering tortoises.

In time, Darwin would study them all, but for now it was the small fluttering finches pecking at insects on the ground that fascinated him. These birds existed in England but he could never have got so close to them. On the Galapagos Islands, the animals had not learned to fear humans because no humans lived here. The finches hopped and pecked happily near his boots. With such a close view, he could see that these finches were not quite like the English ones, and though every one of the Galapagos Islands had finches, they were different on each island too.

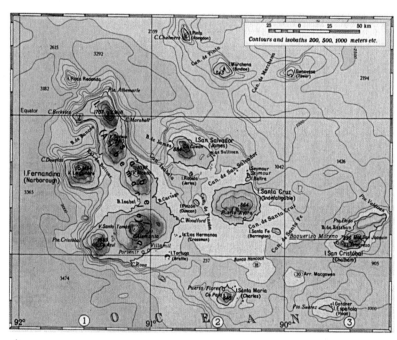

↑ The Galapagos Islands lie 500 miles off the coast of South America. They are separated from one another by deep water. The animals cannot move between the islands to breed, so each island's animals have evolved separately.

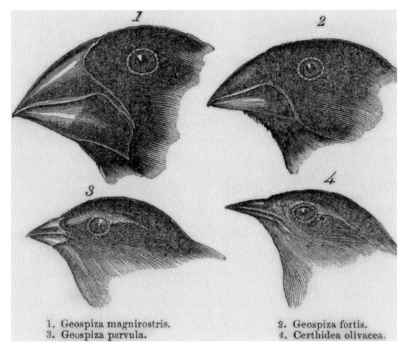

1. Geospiza magnirostris.
2. Geospiza fortis.
3. Geospiza parvula.
4. Certhidea olivacea.

↑ Here are four of Darwin's finches – the large ground finch, the medium ground finch, the small tree finch and the green warbler finch. Each has a differently shaped beak, which has evolved to take advantage of the food nearby.

↑ The Galapagos tortoise is a giant species of tortoise that can live for over 100 years. It makes its home in the wild only on the Galapagos Islands. Darwin noticed that tortoises on the different islands had differently shaped shells.

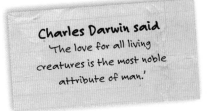

Charles Darwin said
'The love for all living creatures is the most noble attribute of man.'

Darwin crouched down to get closer. As he suspected, it was the shape of the beaks that were different. The finches he was looking at had long pointed beaks, which were ideal for picking up tiny insects. On another island, covered in juicy green plants, the finches had big beaks so that they could bite off large chunks of leaf. On a third island, he had seen finches with powerful beaks for cracking open hard seeds. Darwin stood up and gazed around the strange landscape. Now he was sure – all the plants and animals around him on the islands had developed to make the best use of the food supplies here.

After his travels, Darwin put together the history of finches. Long ago, finches had looked quite different than they do now. And in a family of newly-hatched birds, each member was slightly different – just as human brothers and sisters were different. One bird would have a slightly bigger beak. Another would have a stronger or longer beak. From time to time, a bird would be born with a beak that was better at dealing with the food available. This variation was the key. Darwin realized that all today's plants and animals, including humans, had adapted to suit their surroundings. They had evolved over millions of years from far simpler ancient creatures that were now long-dead.

↑ The peppered moth comes in both dark and light forms. When its habitat was polluted by smoke in the 19th century, the dark form became more common: it blended in with the soot-covered trees and avoided being eaten by other animals.

THE THEORY OF EVOLUTION

▶▶ How would Darwin prove that living things evolve over millions of years?

Darwin's idea that humans and monkeys had evolved from a common, ape-like animal meant he was often mocked in cartoons, such as this. 'Light will be thrown on the origin of man,' responded Darwin.

The cheetah is the fastest of all land mammals. This means it is more likely to catch its prey than slower animals. The cheetah's speed is the result of evolution – over time the cheetah has grown faster.

The Cactus finch is one of Darwin's finches. Its long pointed beak allows it to peck between the sharp cactus spines and pick off insects to eat.

Darwin also noticed something else about the finches – there were more than two eggs in each nest. This meant there would be more chicks than parents. If all the female chicks grew up to lay their own eggs, there would be more and more birds. Over a few generations, the number of finches would increase enormously. Soon, there would be too many birds for the amount of food available, so some would starve. Most often it would be the ones with the best-shaped beaks that survived. He called this 'natural selection'.

But it wasn't just the beaks! Finally, he realized that given enough time, animals and plants could change greatly. Over many generations, animals evolved until they were better suited to the food available. Every living thing was adapted, or suited, to the place in which it lived.

A WORLD-CHANGING IDEA	1831 December	1832 January	1833 August	1835 February
All the evidence Darwin needed to develop his scientific breakthrough came from his long voyage around the world, but he waited more than 20 years before publishing his theory of evolution in full.	Sets sail on the HMS *Beagle* toward South America on a scientific research mission.	At the Cape Verde Islands, off the coast of Africa, becomes convinced the Earth is very old.	In Argentina, discovers the fossil, or preserved remains, of a prehistoric ground sloth.	Escapes injury in an earthquake. It confirms to Darwin that the Earth's surface changes over time.

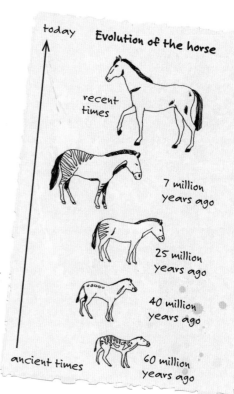

After leaving the Galapagos Islands, Darwin's long voyage continued. He visited many more small islands as well as Australia and Africa before finally arriving back in England. The journey took nearly five years. At home, Darwin wrote books and reports about his findings and discussed them with many other scientists, but he put off publishing his full theory of evolution by many years. This was partly because he knew that he would upset many religious people, including his wife, for suggesting that the story in the Bible about how life was created, was wrong.

In 1859, Darwin finally published his theory of evolution in a famous book called *On the Origin of Species*. There was even more fuss than he had feared. But today, Darwin's ideas form the main basis of all life sciences and he is known as one of the world's greatest scientists.

↑ Today's horses evolved from smaller animals, which once had five toes. Gradually, the middle toe became a hoof and the others disappeared, which helped horses to run better.

↑ Darwin received a letter from a scientist who had come up with his own theory of evolution. After that, he published *On the Origin of Species* as soon as he could.

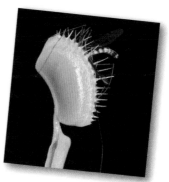

↑ Darwin filled his greenhouse with flesh-eating plants and played music to worms to see whether they responded to vibrations!

1835 March	1835 September	1835 October	1836 January	1836 October	1859 November
Is bitten by a Benchuca bug which he then keeps as a pet, allowing it to suck his blood!	Reaches the volcanic Galapagos Islands. He meets and rides on giant tortoises.	Notices the Galapagos finches and how their beaks suit their food supply.	In Australia, sees a platypus – it is so strange he believes it must have evolved separately from European species.	Arrives in England after a voyage of four years, nine months and five days.	Publishes his theory of evolution in full in *On the Origin of Species*.

UNMASKING
DINOSAURS

SCIENTIFIC AIMS	▶▶ To spot and group together the strange old bones that were regularly being discovered in the 19th century.
CHALLENGES ///////////////////////////// Dealing with unknown species; no modern-day technology or tools to date the finds	**WHO RICHARD OWEN** **WHERE** London and Oxford **WHEN** 1830s to 1840s **METHOD** Measured and compared the bone structures of hundreds of different creatures, including animals that were still living and those that had died out and become extinct.
RESULTS	Owen confirmed that a long-extinct group of reptiles lay buried in the ground. Their remains were preserved as fossils. He called the creatures 'dinosaurs', giving a name to a new group of reptiles.

LIFETIME ACHIEVEMENTS

No. 1 Identified many kinds of creatures that had died out. These included over a dozen types of dinosaur.

No. 2 Founded the mighty Natural History Museum in London, which opened in 1881.

No. 3 Helped by sculptor Benjamin Hawkins, produced the first life-size models of dinosaurs.

NAME: Richard Owen
BORN: July 20th, 1804
DIED: age 88
NATIONALITY: British
JOB: Studying fossils
FAMOUS FOR: Coming up with the term 'dinosaur' which means 'terrible lizard'

→ Richard Owen realized that the fragment of bone he'd been sent must have come from a large bird. He was later sent collections of bird bones and managed to reconstruct the whole skeleton of the extinct Moa bird!

UNMASKING DINOSAURS

▶▶ Owen's study of the huge fossilized bones revealed an incredible secret.

At the age of 23, Richard Owen was put in charge of identifying and cataloguing the Hunterian Collection: an enormous, unruly assortment of over 13,000 dead animal specimens. Owen was a natural, and by the late 1830s he was known as the man to see if you discovered an unusual fossil or a strange bone. Owen was fascinated by his work and remarkably skilful at identifying creatures from just a fragment of their skeletons.

Around the same time, the bones of bizarre creatures were being unearthed by fossil hunters such as William Buckland and Gideon Mantell. Mantell discovered the Iguanodon and Buckland Megalosaurus. All kinds of wild guesses were made about what sort of creatures these might have been. The most common theory was that they were giant lizards. Intrigued by these discoveries, Owen visited Buckland in Oxford. He looked closely at the finds with a powerful new microscope. By studying how the animals' teeth were worn down, he worked out whether the animals had eaten plants or meat while they had been alive.

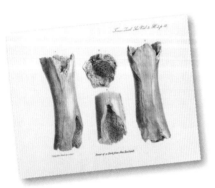

↑ In 1839, Owen examined this 6-inch long section of bone sent to him from New Zealand. Noting that inside it was full of holes, like a honeycomb, he identified it as the legbone of a 6.5-foot tall bird that was long-dead, and had never been seen before.

↑ A drawing of the giant bird Owen named Dinornis, also known as the Giant Moa. Owen was ridiculed at the time for suggesting this bird once lived, but a complete Dinornis skeleton, shown on the previous page, turned up four years later! This proved that his theory was correct.

↑ A dinosaur sculpture designed by Benjamin Waterhouse Hawkins with help from Owen. This sculpture, along with several others, was displayed at the 1851 Great Exhibition in Crystal Palace, London. The sculptures still prowl in a park there today.

→ An idea for the floor plan of the Natural History Museum, as sketched by Richard Owen.

↑ Owen spent much of his later career building the Natural History Museum in London, which he called 'a cathedral to nature'. It featured this Triceratops skeleton among its thousands of exhibits.

In the winter of 1841, news of an unusual find reached Owen. He raced to London to see the fossils and identified them quickly. They were part of the backbone, or spine, of an Iguanodon and were made of a number of bones fused together. In a flash he recalled the Megalosaurus he'd seen in Oxford. The bones in its spine were fused in a similar way.

Working feverishly in his study, Owen figured out that fused lower spines meant that these creatures' strong bodies and pillar-like legs could support enormous weights. The little lizards of recent centuries slither on their bellies, legs splayed out to the sides. These fossil creatures were different! Owen grouped the finds together and realized they were reptiles that had lived on land but had died out. He named them 'dinosaurs' after the Greek words 'deinos', terrible, and 'sauros', lizard. His findings caused a sensation and made him world famous.

EXTRA

SCIENTIFIC SURPRISES

Check out some of the more unusual things Richard Owen got up to in the name of science.

As a surgeon's apprentice, Owen once took a deceased prisoner's head home to study. A few years later, he brought back part of a dead and smelly elephant to cut up.

Owen was the first to describe the prehistoric bird Archaeopteryx but he got the parts mixed up. He also thought that Iguanodon had a spike on its snout. It turned out that the spike was actually on its thumb!

In 1853, Owen hosted a dinner party for scientists. To make it exciting, he held it inside the belly of a giant dinosaur model.

DRIFTING
CONTINENTS

SCIENTIFIC AIMS	▶▶ To discover how the Earth changed over billions of years. To untangle the ancient history of the land masses, or continents.
CHALLENGES ///////////////////////////////// The scientific world disagreed with him; he could say what had happened but not why	**WHO ALFRED WEGENER** **WHERE** Berlin **WHEN** 1911 to 1930 **METHOD** Studied how continents, such as Europe, had moved over billions of years. He identified preserved animal remains called fossils that showed some continents had once been side by side.
RESULTS	Showed that it was very likely that the continents were once joined together and have since drifted apart over billions of years. The process is known as continental drift and still continues today.

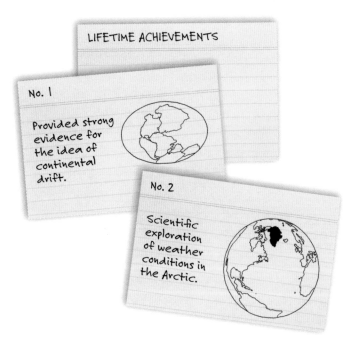

LIFETIME ACHIEVEMENTS

No. 1

Provided strong evidence for the idea of continental drift.

No. 2

Scientific exploration of weather conditions in the Arctic.

NAME: Alfred Lothar Wegener
BORN: November 1st 1880
DIED: age 50
NATIONALITY: German
JOB: meteorologist
FAMOUS FOR: proposing the idea of continental drift and his polar research

→ In 1930, Wegener set out on his fourth and final expedition to Greenland, to set up a base camp where the Arctic weather could be studied. He never came home.

DRIFTING CONTINENTS

▶▶ Would anyone believe Wegener's ideas about how the Earth had changed?

Alfred Wegener was dying, far from home in a world of ice. His thoughts turned, as they so often did, to his discovery. He knew that if the world's continents were gathered together, they would fit neatly, like the pieces of a jigsaw. He remembered the long years of collecting evidence to prove that the coastlines, now far distant, were once side by side. As he closed his eyes for the last time, he wondered again: would anyone ever believe him?

↑ This photo of Wegener and his colleague Rasmus Villumsen was taken on his fourth expedition to Greenland. They left for their base camp the next day, but Wegener died of a heart attack and Villumsen disappeared in the snow.

↑ In 1930, on Wegener's final Greenland expedition, vital supplies were carried by dog sleds. But due to bad weather conditions, the trip ended in tragedy.

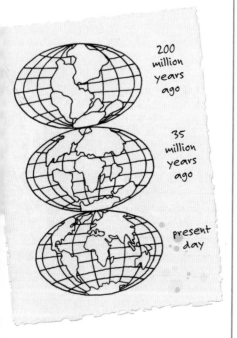

200 million years ago

35 million years ago

present day

↑ This diagram shows how Earth's continents were once joined but have moved apart, illustrating Wegener's ideas about continental drift.

Wegener's death, at the age of 50, was the end of an active life. In his twenties, along with his older brother Kurt, he had been the first to explore the air and weather in balloons. Wegener later took part in four scientific expeditions to snowbound Greenland, mainly to study the science of weather. In World War I, he fought at the front. Too badly wounded to continue, he worked for the military weather service and wrote up his ideas about continental drift in a book called *The Origin of Continents and Oceans.*

Wegener's idea was hard to accept because no one had any idea how continents could drift apart. After all, the Earth is a giant ball of rock and metal, so people believed the continents were firmly fixed in place.

↑ The Himalayan mountains are the highest in the world. They were formed when two of the Earth's plates were pressed together, making the crust buckle.

Some scientists suggested that the surface of the Earth might be made up of a few huge 'plates', which floated on an underground sea of molten rock. The idea was that each continent was perched on one of these plates, which themselves extended beneath the oceans, so that they touched each other. But it was hard to see how the plates could move. It was not until the 1960s that studies of the ocean floor uncovered good evidence for this idea. We now know that at some places the edges of the continental plates are being formed and at others they are being destroyed, or crumpling up. They move because of the motions of the melted rock beneath, like the bubbles at the top of a pan of heated soup.

↑ Wherever the Earth's plates crush together or tear apart, volcanoes or earthquakes can happen. When a volcano erupts, the hot rock under the Earth finds its way to the surface and pours down the sides of the volcano as lava.

↑ Two continental plates meet in a curving boundary line that runs up the Atlantic Ocean. In Iceland, this boundary is on land, where it is marked by rift valleys like this one, where the Earth's surface has been pulled apart.

↑ Wegener's idea that today's continents were once joined was supported by his discovery that now-distant places have similar fossils. Traces of this creature, Cynognathus, have been found in both South America and Africa.

DEFINING OUR SOLAR SYSTEM

SCIENTIFIC AIMS	▶▶ To persuade people that the Sun, not the Earth, was at the center of our group of planets, which we call the solar system.
CHALLENGES ///////////////////////////// The telescope had not then been invented; his ideas were not accepted in his lifetime	**WHO** **NICOLAUS COPERNICUS** **WHERE** Krakow, Poland **WHEN** 1504 to 1543 **METHOD** Studied the skies and made mathematical models. Copernicus assumed that the Sun was at the center of the solar system, then worked out how the planets moved around it.
RESULTS	Copernicus thought that the planets moved in fixed circles. He was wrong about this but his basic idea that the Earth and other planets traveled around, or orbited, the Sun was correct.

LIFETIME ACHIEVEMENTS

No. 1

Argued that the Earth and other planets moved around the Sun.

No. 2

Defended his town from attack by ferocious warring knights.

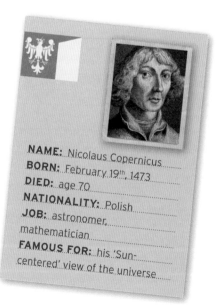

NAME: Nicolaus Copernicus
BORN: February 19th, 1473
DIED: age 70
NATIONALITY: Polish
JOB: astronomer, mathematician
FAMOUS FOR: his 'Sun-centered' view of the universe

→ Copernicus uses a pair of compasses to compare his measurements of the planets against his map of the solar system.

DEFINING OUR
SOLAR SYSTEM

▶▶ **Copernicus was sure that the experts were wrong about the solar system.**

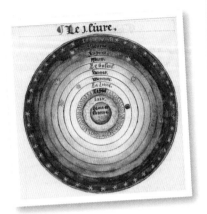

↑ This illustration shows the solar system as astronomers believed it to be during Copernicus's lifetime. The Earth is at the center with the Sun, Moon and other planets going around it.

↑ Copernicus used an armillary sphere like this one to measure the positions of the stars and planets.

↑ This statue of Copernicus stands in Warsaw, the capital city of Poland.

↑ According to Copernicus, the Sun was at the center of the solar system and the planets, such as Earth, traveled around it. Only the Moon went around the Earth.

Copernicus leafed through the thick pile of handwritten sheets. He asked himself a question that he had asked many times before – should he publish his work? Nearly forty years ago, he had decided that the popular view about the universe was wrong. The Earth was not fixed and static at the center of the universe. Since then, he had worked out and written down the details of his own theory. He believed that the Earth and the other planets traveled around the Sun. He also believed that every day the Earth turned once on its axis, which is an imaginary line running through the center of the Earth.

Cautiously, Copernicus discussed his ideas with trusted colleagues. Most agreed with him, including fellow mathematician Georg Rheticus, who had even printed a summary of his theory. So what made Copernicus hesitate to tell people that they lived on a moving planet? It was the all-powerful Catholic Church. Copernicus was a priest and he knew the Church would disagree strongly. He dreaded to think what they might do but he knew he had to tell the truth.

↑ Copernicus did not use a telescope. He used a triquetrum, which is the rod on the right of the picture. This device measured the heights of stars and planets. In the background is Frombork Cathedral, where Copernicus served as a priest.

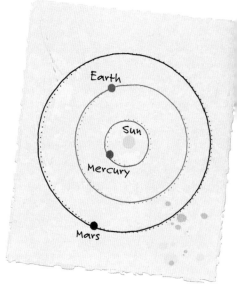

↑ Copernicus made one big error. He said that the planets traveled around the Sun in circles. They actually follow elliptical, or oval, paths. In this diagram, the dotted lines show Copernicus's circular paths and the colored lines show the actual paths of three planets.

Although Copernicus did not live to see it, his ideas changed the way we look at the world forever. In 1543, just before his death, he finally published his book *On the Revolutions of the Heavenly Spheres*. It encouraged other scientists, including Galileo Galilei (see pages 78–83), to investigate the solar system and eventually prove that Copernicus was correct. Copernicus knew the Catholic Church rejected his theory and did its best to silence those who believed in it. But today, we know the Earth is not at the center of the solar system. It does indeed go around the Sun.

Copernicus did not spend all his time studying astronomy. He was a priest in the cathedral of Frombork, in Poland, and had many duties. In 1519, a vicious war broke out between Poland and a mighty group of German knights called the Teutonic Order. They attacked Fromberg and burnt down many buildings, including Copernicus's home. He fled to the nearby city of Olsztyn and was asked to take charge. Over several months, Copernicus built up the town's defenses. When the knights attacked the following year, he saved the city from defeat!

↑ This is Olsztyn Castle, where Copernicus lived and worked. He helped to save the castle and town from fierce bombardment.

LOOKING INTO SPACE

SCIENTIFIC AIMS	▶▶ To prove that the Earth traveled around the Sun, not the other way around as people at the time believed.
CHALLENGES /////////////////////// His work went against religious teachings, and there was the threat of arrest and torture	**WHO** GALILEO GALILEI **WHERE** Padua and Tuscany **WHEN** 1609 to the 1620s **METHOD** Built telescopes and observed the planets. Galileo also investigated Earth's tides. He thought that they existed because the Earth was moving but this idea was wrong.
RESULTS	Galileo discovered moons traveling around the planet Jupiter, which made him realize that not everything circled the Earth. This helped him argue that the Sun was at the center of the solar system.

LIFETIME ACHIEVEMENTS

No. 1
Discovered objects in space and was first to draw the rugged surface of the Moon.

No. 2
Developed rules describing how objects move and fall to Earth.

No. 3
Worked out how to use a pendulum, which is a swinging weight, to improve the accuracy of clocks.

NAME: Galileo Galilei
BORN: February 15th, 1564
DIED: age 77
NATIONALITY: Italian
JOB: astronomer, physicist
FAMOUS FOR: discovering the moons of Jupiter – Io, Europa, Callisto and Ganymede

→ Galileo holds up a sketch of the features of the Moon while a cardinal looks on in disbelief. Galileo made the sketch using observations from his telescope.

LOOKING INTO SPACE

▶▶ Could Galileo prove the order of the solar system?

↑ This is a drawing from Galileo's book *Starry Message* showing his sketches of the Moon. From the shadows they cast, Galileo guessed that the mountains on the Moon were over 3 miles high.

↑ The telescope was invented in 1608, probably in Holland. The fame of the invention spread rapidly, and within a few months Galileo had built much better versions of his own based on vague descriptions of the original.

Galileo raised the telescope to his right eye and covered the other. His first target was obvious – the Moon. This was a body thought perfectly smooth by astronomers and churchmen. At first, he could see only a wash of white light so he adjusted the telescope slightly. Suddenly a landscape swam into focus, a world of black and white. Could this really be the Moon? As he moved the telescope slowly he saw it shared some of the same features as Earth, including winding valleys, vast rocky mountains and flat plains.

Enthralled, he looked elsewhere at the heavens. The white smear of the Milky Way Galaxy showed itself to be a made up of thousands of tiny stars. The distant planet Saturn was not round at all. Then he saw its neighbor, Jupiter. What were those tiny points of light nearby? At the time, the common belief was that the Earth was at the center of the solar system, and everything circled around it. However these points of light seemed to be orbiting Jupiter just as the Moon orbited the Earth. If they really were moons circling another planet, then that changed everything.

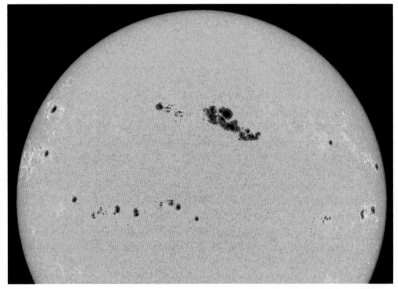

↑ Galileo used his telescope to watch sunspots – dark, cooler areas on surface of the Sun. The movement of the spots suggested that the Sun spun on its axis, an invisible line running down through its center.

As he investigated further, Galileo became convinced. His discovery agreed with the ideas of Nicolaus Copernicus, who was an astronomer and mathematician who had lived a century before (see pages 72–77). Galileo was determined to speak out for this new truth, despite the dangerous fact that it flatly disagreed with the views of the Church.

↑ In 1633, the astronomer was forced to deny his discoveries. Here Galileo faces Father Firenzuola, the head of the Roman Inquisition.

The result was one of the most important books ever written: *Dialogues Concerning the Two Chief World Systems*. One of these systems had the Sun and planets traveling around the Earth, the other said the Earth and other planets went around the Sun. The second system was the one Copernicus had believed was right. The book made it clear that Galileo agreed.

Unfortunately for Galileo, the Pope, who is the leader of the Catholic Church, had allowed the book to be written in the first place only if it did *not* conclude that Copernicus was right. As a result, Galileo was summoned and tried by the Roman Inquisition. He was threatened with torture, forced to state that he was wrong, forbidden to write about such matters again and sentenced to house arrest for the rest of his days.

▶▶ Could Galileo prove the order of the solar system?

Galileo's punishments did not stop him from working and he published another book, *Two New Sciences*, which explained his discoveries in many fields of physics, including motion, optics, which is the study of light, acoustics, which is the study of sound, and engineering.

Some of these discoveries were as important as his new view of the solar system. Until Galileo, people had thought that heavy objects fell faster than light ones. Galileo corrected this error, showing that all objects should fall at the same speed whatever their mass, which is the amount of matter or 'stuff' they contain. The reason some objects on Earth fall more slowly is that they experience air resistance, or 'drag'. This is why a parachute falls slowly. Drag also means that a cannonball fired through the air slows down faster and curves back to Earth sooner than if there were no air.

↑ Galileo imagined two objects of different mass, which is the amount of matter or 'stuff' they contain, falling from Italy's Tower of Pisa. He knew that only the drag of air resistance stopped them from hitting the ground at the same time.

↑ In 1972, Apollo astronaut David R. Scott showed that Galileo's idea worked. While on the Moon he dropped a feather and a hammer at the same time. There is no air on the Moon. The feather and the hammer landed at the same time.

↑ Galileo, sitting on the right, was confined to a villa in Florence, Italy. Here he talks to the mathematician and engineer Vincenzo Viviani, who assisted him.

Galileo was an inventor as well as a scientist. He worked out how to build his telescopes using only a vague description of the newly invented device. He also made money by inventing, making, and selling a 'geometrical and military compass' that could measure angles to aim cannons and help astronomers, as well as convert currencies and measure widths.

↑ It's said that Galileo became interested in how things swing while watching a lamp in Pisa cathedral. He used his heartbeat to time it moving back and forth.

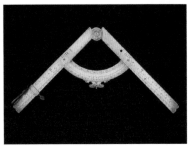

↑ This is the geometric and military compass Galileo invented. With the help of the craftsman Marc'Antonio Mazzoleni he made and sold over 100 of them.

Galileo continued working even when he became blind. One of his last discoveries was a way of using a pendulum, a weight swinging back and forth, to help a clock keep better time. It was based on something he had noticed decades before, that two pendulums of the same length will take the same amount of time to swing forward and back – even if one is swinging in a longer arc, or has a heavy weight at the end.

Galileo was successful partly because of his determination and brilliance, but also because of the way he worked. He made measurements and observations that were as accurate as possible and he tried to explain things as simply as possible. He tried to express his discoveries in the form of mathematical laws that could be tested and used. All these principles are essential to science today. Many believe that Galileo was the first true scientist.

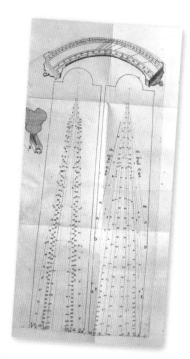

↑ A sketch of the compass from one of Galileo's books. The device was used in calculations until the 19th century.

DISCOVERING GALAXIES

SCIENTIFIC AIMS	▶▶ To work out the size of the universe, which is everything that exists, including planet Earth, the Sun and distant galaxies.
CHALLENGES ///////////////////////////////// His ideas were hard to accept, and many other scientists did not believe him	**WHO** EDWIN HUBBLE **WHERE** Mount Wilson Observatory, California, USA **WHEN** 1922 to 1935 **METHOD** Studied galaxies through a powerful telescope. We live in a galaxy called the Milky Way, which includes the Sun, other stars and the planets.
RESULTS	Hubble discovered that there are many galaxies like our own in the universe, and that they are moving further apart all the time. His investigations made him realize that the universe is getting bigger.

LIFETIME ACHIEVEMENTS

No. 1
Helped to prove that the universe is expanding, or getting bigger.

No. 2
Discovered that our Galaxy, the Milky Way, is just one of many.

No. 3
Developed a system to classify galaxies according to their shape.

NAME: Edwin Powell Hubble
BORN: November 20th, 1889
DIED: age 63
NATIONALITY: American
JOB: astronomer, Army major
FAMOUS FOR: showing that the universe contains many galaxies and is expanding

→ Hubble stands next to the giant telescope at Mount Wilson Observatory. He used this telescope to make all his major discoveries.

DISCOVERING GALAXIES

▶▶ Just how big is the universe? Edwin Hubble was about to investigate.

▶▶ HOW TO ...

Search the Night Sky

All you need to explore the universe is a cloudless night and a pair of binoculars.

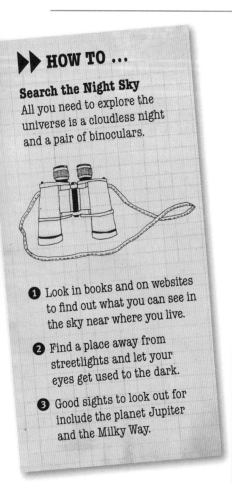

1 Look in books and on websites to find out what you can see in the sky near where you live.

2 Find a place away from streetlights and let your eyes get used to the dark.

3 Good sights to look out for include the planet Jupiter and the Milky Way.

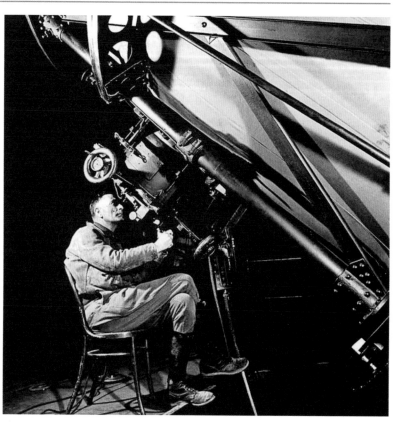

↑ Hubble makes observations at the Mount Wilson observatory in 1937. The telescope seen here is the Hooker telescope, which is 8.2 feet long.

↑ Hubble and his colleagues stand outside the Mount Wilson Observatory where Hubble worked. The domed roof opens so that the telescope inside can view the night sky.

Slowly, Hubble moved his lens across the collection of shiny photographs of the night sky. He had taken them over many weeks. There was one star in particular that fascinated him, changing from dimness to brightness and back again over many days. This star was a star known as Cepheid. Over the next few weeks, Hubble photographed the same part of the night sky again and again through his giant telescope. This meant that he could plot the changes in the brightness of the star. He found that it took 31.4 days for it to go through its changes. This is called the 'period' of the star.

About a decade earlier, an astronomer called Henrietta Leavitt had studied Cepheids and discovered that the brighter a Cepheid is, the longer its period. This meant that Hubble could work out how bright his Cepheid was from its period. A 31.4 day period meant that the star was extremely bright.

DANGER! Studying the sky with binoculars is lots of fun, but don't go out alone at night, and never look directly at the Sun.

But, strangely, this Cepheid looked very dim indeed. If a bright star looks dim then it must be far away. A quick calculation told Hubble that the Cepheid was at least three times further away than the edge of our Galaxy, the Milky Way. Most people thought that the edge of the Milky Way was the edge of the universe. Hubble realized that the universe was bigger than anyone had imagined.

That was just part of Hubble's breakthrough. The Cepheid was one of a group of stars. Previously, astronomers had thought that this star group was located within the Milky Way, but now Hubble knew that the Cepheid and the stars near it must be members of another galaxy. So, there were at least two galaxies in our Universe. Soon it became clear that there are many, many more. We live in a vast universe of galaxies.

↑ The Cepheid that Hubble found is part of the Andromeda Galaxy. This galaxy is over two million light years away from Earth.

EXTRA

SCIENTIST SURPRISES

Here are a few of Hubble's other interests and achievements.

The young Hubble was a talented American football player. His father insisted that he stopped playing because he thought that the game was too dangerous.

Hubble then became a boxer. He was so good that he was offered the chance to train for the World Heavyweight Championship.

Hubble volunteered for the US Army during World War I, and in World War II he became involved in weapons research. In his later years he became completely opposed to war.

DISCOVERING GALAXIES

▶▶ Just how big is the universe? Edwin Hubble was about to investigate.

↑ As part of his work, Hubble developed a classification system for galaxies. He grouped them by their shape. This is a 'barred spiral' galaxy.

↑ Between 1917 and 1948, the telescope at Mount Wilson was the largest in the world. With it, the sizes of stars could be measured for the very first time.

the 'fruit-bread' universe

before

after

↑ This diagram shows what happens to a lump of raisin dough as it expands. Like the raisins, groups of galaxies move away from distant groups faster than they do from near neighbors.

Along with the scientist Georges Lemaître (see pages 90–91) and several other astronomers, Hubble also contributed to one of the greatest discoveries ever made in astronomy. Together they realized that galaxies are moving away from us and that the more distant a galaxy is, the faster it is moving away. This means that the whole universe is expanding, or getting bigger. At the time this was a completely new idea!

Galaxies form groups in space. The groups move faster as they get further apart. Imagine that the universe is a lump of fruit bread dough and that the raisins scattered in the dough are groups of galaxies. As the yeast makes the dough expand, the raisins move apart. The raisins that are far away from each other move apart more quickly than the raisins that are close together.

Not everyone accepted Hubble's ideas. Another great astronomer at the time was Harlow Shapley. Shapley had recently put forward his own model of the universe. It was much smaller than Hubble's, and in his model there was nothing beyond the Milky Way. In 1923, Hubble wrote to Shapley and explained his findings, proving that Shapley's model was wrong. Shapely showed the letter to a friend and said, 'Here is the letter that has destroyed my universe.'

Hubble spent most of his later life developing bigger and better telescopes. He was very involved with the building of a giant telescope at Mount Palomar in California, USA. He continued to study galaxies when he could. A galaxy spins around, and Hubble was interested in how the stars in a galaxy are affected by these rotations. Hubble was also keen to make people treat astronomy as a proper science. In his lifetime, astronomers could not be nominated for the Nobel Prize, which is one of the highest awards a scientist can achieve. The rule did change but only after Hubble's death. The Nobel prize is just awarded to living scientists, and so Hubble never won.

Together with Georges Lemaître and other astronomers, Hubble entirely changed our understanding of the universe. Not only did they show that it was much larger than people thought, but also that it was changing and growing. One hundred and one years after Hubble's birth, a telescope was named after him and launched into space. It proved to be one of the most successful space telescopes ever, providing us with pictures of other planets, stars and galaxies. It has added greatly to our knowledge of the larger and stranger universe that Hubble discovered.

↑ In 1990, the space shuttle *Discovery* delivered the Hubble Space Telescope into orbit. Three years later, the shuttle *Endeavour* visited the telescope to repair a fault.

↑ This image, taken by the Hubble Space Telescope, shows the Pillars of Creation. This is a part of our Galaxy where new stars are being born in vast dust clouds.

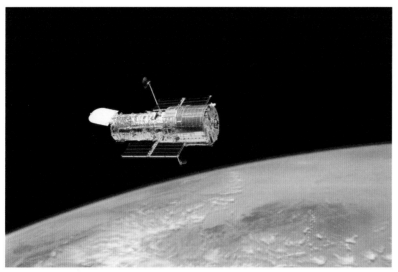

↑ The Hubble Space Telescope drifts high above the Earth. It takes breathtaking photographs of objects in space. It also provides astronomers with information that they use to develop Edwin Hubble's work.

↑ The Eta Carinae nebula, or dust cloud, shown here in a photograph from the Hubble Space Telescope. It contains two of the brightest and most massive stars known.

THE BIG BANG

SCIENTIFIC AIMS	▶▶ To explain how the universe began. The universe is everything that exists. It includes all the planets, stars and galaxies.
CHALLENGES / His work went unnoticed for several years; scientists did not always trust his ideas	**WHO GEORGES LEMAÎTRE** **WHERE** Belgium **WHEN** 1923 to 1932 **METHOD** Lemaître used the work of the physicist Albert Einstein (see pages 40–43) and the astronomer Edwin Hubble (see pages 84–89) to help develop his own ideas.
RESULTS	Lemaître was the first person to show that billions of years ago the universe suddenly expanded from a hot and dense state. This idea for the start of the universe became known as the Big Bang theory.

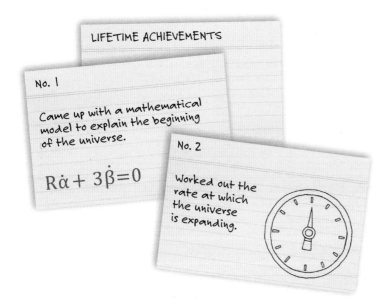

LIFETIME ACHIEVEMENTS

No. 1

Came up with a mathematical model to explain the beginning of the universe.

$$R\dot\alpha + 3\dot\beta = 0$$

No. 2

Worked out the rate at which the universe is expanding.

NAME: Georges Henri Joseph Édouard Lemaître
BORN: July 17th, 1894
DIED: age 71
NATIONALITY: Belgian
JOB: astronomer, mathematician
FAMOUS FOR: his work on how the universe formed, or began

→ Lemaître was both a Catholic priest and a scientist. He joined together ideas of science and religion, which made some scientists nervous.

THE BIG BANG

▶▶ Could Lemaître really explain how the universe began?

↑ When World War I broke out in 1914, Lemaître was at university, studying engineering. He abandoned his studies to join the Belgian Army.

Georges Lemaître said
'The evolution of the universe can be likened to a display of fireworks that has just ended: some few red wisps, ashes and smoke.'

↑ Einstein, left, talks with Lemaître. Although they did not agree about the details of the universe, they thought highly of each other. Support from Einstein helped Lemaître to win several honors.

↑ This picture shows galaxies in a distant part of the universe. The light that we see in the picture has been traveling for billions of years. This photo shows how galaxies looked billions of years ago, not long after the universe was formed.

Georges Lemaître wasn't happy, even though everyone thought he should be. Arthur Eddington, an astronomer and a friend, had told everyone about a scientific paper Lemaître had written four years ago. Soon Lemaître was famous as the man who had found a way to make Albert Einstein's powerful model of the universe fit Edwin Hubble's incredible discovery that the universe was expanding.

But Lemaître was unhappy about the picture his model painted of the beginning of the universe. He had imagined that the early universe would look like it does today but would be much smaller. But how had that early, smaller universe begun?

If, as Hubble said, the universe was expanding, then long ago it must have been relatively small and very compact indeed. Lemaître realized that simplicity was the key. A universe, even a small one, was an extremely complex thing. But what if the universe had started out simply, not in a complex way?

The simplest thing Lemaître knew was the atom, which is a tiny building block of matter. He thought hard. Perhaps the universe began with just one atom rather than trillions of atoms as he had first imagined. If so, this atom would have to be far larger than the Sun and contain the mass of the whole universe. It was hard to see how such an atom could be stable... and that was the final piece of the puzzle. That kind of atom could *not* be stable. As soon as this 'super atom' appeared it would explode. Lemaître picked up his pen. It was time to do some math.

The idea Lemaître developed is now known as the Big Bang theory. It explains that the universe began in a very hot state. It expanded suddenly and it is still expanding. Today, we know Lemaître was right except for one thing. At the earliest stage, all the matter in the universe was not in one 'super atom', but it was compacted to just a few millimeters across. What we don't know is what will happen to the universe in the future. The two main theories are that it will either go on expanding forever, or that everything in it, galaxies, stars, planets, even the atoms, will eventually tear themselves apart.

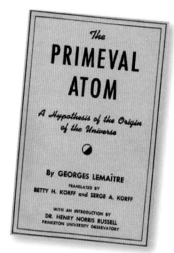

↑ In 1946, Lemaître published a book to explain his theory about the universe. It was called *The Primeval Atom*. Lemaître described that imaginary first atom as the 'Cosmic Egg', but the term never caught on!

↑ This is an array, or group, of radio telescopes in California, USA. They measure energy traveling in the form of radiation, known as radio waves. The telescopes have shown that the energy produced by the Big Bang still exists, helping to prove that Lemaître's ideas were correct.

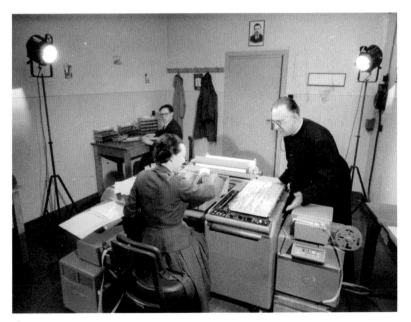

↑ Lemaître was one of the first astronomers to use a computers for his calculations. This is the E101 computer at the university where he worked.

GLOSSARY

ancestor
A relative from whom you are descended, such as your great-grandfather.

antibiotic
A drug such as penicillin used to kill bacteria (germs) and cure an infection.

astronomy
The study of everything in space.

atmosphere
A layer of gases around a planet or star. The Earth has an atmosphere.

atom
The smallest unit of a chemical element, too small to see, from which everything is made.

bacteria
A type of germ. Many bacteria are harmless, or even helpful, but some give us diseases.

biology
The study of living things.

blood vessels
Tubes that carry blood around your body.

characteristic
Something that helps to identify an object, person or animal.

chemistry
The study of different substances and how they react and change.

circulation
Going around and around. Blood circulates around the body.

classify
To decide which group something belongs to. A dog is classified as a member of the group of animals called mammals.

continent
A huge mass of land on Earth. The continents are Africa, North and South America, Antarctica, Asia, Australia and Europe.

continental drift
The extremely slow movement of the continental plates toward or away from each other.

continental plate
A giant slab of the Earth's crust (the outer layer of the Earth) on which one or more continents sit.

DNA
A chemical found in every living thing, short for Deoxyribonucleic Acid. It contains the information needed for living things to live and grow.

drag
In science, drag is the pulling back of a moving object by the air or water it moves through.

eclipse
The blocking of one object in space by another so that the light is cut off. When the Moon cuts off the light from the Sun, it is called a solar eclipse.

electricity
The energy that travels along wires to make lights, TVs and other things work. Lightning is also a kind of electricity.

electromagnetism
A type of energy that can appear as magnetism or electricity.

element
A substance that is made from just one kind of atom, and cannot be broken down into anything simpler. Salt is made out of two elements, sodium and chlorine.

energy
What makes things happen. Motion (movement), light, heat, sound, electricity and magnetism are kinds of energy. Energy can change from one form to another but cannot be destroyed.

equation
A mathematical statement that says that something is equal to something else, such as $12 = 2 \times 6$.

evolution
The idea that one type of living thing develops and changes into another type over millions of years.

extinct
No longer alive and with no living members on Earth. For example, dinosaurs are extinct.

germ
A tiny microscopic thing that causes disease. They are divided into bacteria and viruses.

formula
A kind of equation that shows you how to work something out.

fossil
Traces of a dead plant or animal from long ago, preserved in rock.

galaxy
A vast group of stars. Our Galaxy is called the Milky Way and contains the Sun along with roughly 200 billion other stars.

gene
One of the parts of a living cell whose job is to pass on characteristics such as eye color from parents to their children.

geometry
The area of mathematics that deals with shapes.

gravity
The force that pulls one object toward another one. Gravity pulls you to the ground and keeps the Moon going around the Earth.

infection
The process by which germs give someone a disease. A disease caused by germs is also called an infection.

magnet
A piece of metal, such as iron, that pulls other metals toward it.

mass
A measure of the amount of 'stuff' in an object. The more massive an object is, the more it weighs.

microbe
A living thing that can be seen only with a microscope. If a microbe causes disease, it's called a germ.

microbiology
The study of living things that can only be seen with a microscope.

microscopic
Describes an object that can be seen only with a microscope.

mineral
A solid substance, that occurs naturally in the Earth. It may be a single element, such as gold, or it may be a mixture of several.

model
A lot of scientists build models. A model may show the universe, a complicated molecule like DNA or even how an animal grows.

molecule
Two or more atoms joined together. A molecule of water is made of two atoms of hydrogen joined to one atom of oxygen.

nebula
A vast cloud-like shape, either dark or glowing, far away in space. Most nebulae are made of dust or gas.

orbit
The path of one object around another one in space.

particle
A tiny object. Molecules, atoms and electrons are all particles.

penicillin
A type of antibiotic. It was the first useful antibiotic to be found and is still used widely today.

periodic table
A table in which all the elements are positioned according to their properties (characteristics).

physics
The study of matter (the 'stuff' things are made of) and energy.

quantum
A tiny 'lump' of energy. The plural is quanta.

radiation
The process by which particles or forms of energy travel. The particles or energy are also called radiation.

radioactivity
The release of any of three powerful kinds of radiation called alpha, beta and gamma rays.

relativity
A successful theory explaining how time, mass, energy, space and gravity are connected.

solar system
The Sun, and all the things that go around it, including the Earth and the rest of the planets.

species
A group of living things of the same kind. Cats are an example of a species.

theory
A scientific idea which has been tested and found to work well.

universe
Everything that exists.

vaccine
A medicine designed to fight a virus.

virus
A complicated chemical that may cause a disease. Colds and flu are caused by viruses.

INDEX

a = above; b = below; l = left; r = right; c = center

Chapter Icons: *Medicine, Matter and Energy* Sam Toon/iStockphoto.com *Human Body* Bubaone/iStockphoto.com *Planet Earth, The Universe* Brown Dog Studios/iStockphoto.com; Pages 2 Yves Grosdidier (University of Montreal and Observatoire de Strasbourg), Anthony Moffat (University of Montreal), Gilles Joncas (University Laval), Agnes Acker (Observatoire de Strasbourg), and NASA 4al (petri dish) Don Stalons/Centers for Disease Control and Prevention, Atlanta 4al (engraving) from William Harvey, *Exercitatio Anatomica de Motu Cordis et Sanguinis in Animalibus*, 1628 4bl (Curie) Bibliothèque Nationale de France, Paris 4bl (Newton) Lebrecht Music and Arts Photo Library/Alamy 5ar (dinosaurs) Bill Varie/Corbis 5ar (moon) from Galileo Galilei, *Sidereus Nuncius*, 1610 5bl (Hubble) Huntington Library/SuperStock 5bl (nebula) C.R. O'Dell and S.K. Wong (Rice University)/NASA 7a (Pasteur) Smithsonian Institution, Washington, D.C. 7a (Crick & Watson) Bettmann/Corbis 7a (Curie) Bibliothèque Nationale de France, Paris 7a (Darwin) Down House, Kent 7a (Hubble), 8br Library of Congress, Washington, D.C. 9 Rijksmuseum, Amsterdam 10cl Joel Yale/Time Life Pictures/Getty Images 10ac Blue Lantern Studio/Corbis 10bl Ann Ronan Picture Library/Scala Archives 11cra iStockphoto/Thinkstock.com 11crb Dorling Kindersley RF/Thinkstock.com 11bl Mix Rinho/Shutterstock.com 11br S. Muay/Shutterstock.com 12br George Grantham Bain Collection/Library of Congress, Washington, D.C. 13 Bettmann/Corbis 14c Mary Evans Picture Library/Alamy 14bl Musée Pasteur de Dole/Dagli Orti/The Art Archive 15a Prisma Archivo/Alamy 15br Science Museum, London/Science & Society Picture Library 16al Hulton-Deutsch Collection/Corbis 16c Prisma/UIG/Getty Images 16bl Deloche/BSIP/SuperStock 17al Prisma/UIG/Getty Images 17ar CDC/BSIP/SuperStock 17br Gamma-Keystone/Getty Images 18br Oscar White/Corbis 19 Alfred Eisenstaedt/Time & Life Pictures/Getty Images 20al Bernd Udo/Shutterstock.com 20bl Daily Herald Archive/National Media Museum/Science & Society Picture Library 20bc Prisma/SuperStock 20cl Popperfoto/Getty Images 21ar U.S. National Archives and Records Administration, Maryland 21br BSIP/SuperStock 22br, 23 © GlaxoSmithKline. Used with permission/Courtesy Estate of Gertrude Elion 24al Vinicius Tupinamba/Dreamstime.com 24ar © GlaxoSmithKline. Used with permission/Courtesy Estate of Gertrude Elion 24bl Richard T. Nowitz/Corbis 25ar Shutterstock.com 25bl © GlaxoSmithKline. Used with permission/Courtesy Estate of Gertrude Elion 25br Will and Deni McIntyre/Time Life Pictures/Getty Images 26br Library of Congress, Washington, D.C. 27 The Art Gallery Collection/Alamy 28ac Yale University Library, Connecticut 28bl from William Harvey, Exercitatio Anatomica de Motu Cordis et Sanguinis in Animalibus, 1628 29al Harris Museum and Art Gallery, Preston 29ar Library of Congress, Washington, D.C. 29br Bibliothèque Nationale de France, Paris 30bl, 30br Bettmann/Corbis 31 A. Barrington Brown/Science Photo Library 32al Wellcome Library, London/Wellcome Images 32bl Bettmann/Corbis 32br Leigh Prather/Shutterstock.com 33ar Sam Yeh/AFP/Getty Images 33cl Jochen Tac/Imagebroker.net/SuperStock 33br Roger Ressmeyer/Corbis 34br National Portrait Gallery, London 35 National Geographic Society/Corbis 36al Image Asset Management Ltd./SuperStock 36cl Private Collection 36c Bridgeman Art Library/Getty Images 37bl Granger Collection/TopFoto 37br Science Archive, Oxford/Scala Archives 38bl from Isaac Newton, *Philosophiae Naturalis Principia Mathematica*, 1687 38br Philippe Lissac/Godong/Corbis 39al Science Museum, London 39ar National Portrait Galley, London 39cr Museum and Art Gallery, Derby 39br Archive of the Berlin-Brandenburg Academy of Sciences and Humanities, Berlin 40br Library of Congress, Washington, D.C. 41 Mondadori Portfolio/The Art Archive 42al akg-images 42ar Science & Society/SuperStock 43ar Bettmann/Corbis 43cr, 43br Mondadori Portfolio/The Art Archive 43bl Stephen Bisgrove/Alamy 44br Bibliothèque Nationale de France, Paris 45 White Images/Scala Archives 46al Ted Kinsman/Science Photo Library 46c akg-images 46bl Bibliothèque Nationale de France, Paris 47al Bettmann/Corbis 47ar Bibliothèque Nationale de France, Paris 47br Library of Congress, Washington, D.C. 48br Science Museum, London/Science & Society Picture Library 49 Fine Art Images/Superstock 50al Science Museum, London/Science & Society Picture Library 50cl © Heinrich Pniok (www.pse-mendelejew.de) 50bl Nuno Andre/Shutterstock.com 50br Julia Reschke/Shutterstock.com 51ar DeGolyer Library, Southern Methodist University, Texas 51cr Private Collection 51br Science Museum, London/Science & Society Picture Library 52br Image Asset Management, Ltd./SuperStock 53 Hulton-Deutsch Collection/Corbis 54ar Chemical Heritage Foundation, Philadelphia 54bl Aixam Mega Ltd. 55ar Stock Montage/Getty Images 55cr Patrick Seeger/EPA/Corbis 55bl Bridgeman Art Library/Getty Images 55br Einar Muoni/Shutterstock.com 56br Bibliothèque Nationale de France, Paris 57 University of Amsterdam 58al Royal Library, Copenhagen 58ar Science Archive, Oxford/Scala Archives 58cl Library of Congress, Washington, D.C. 58bl Shutterstock.com 59bl from Carl Linnaeus, *Flora Lapponica*, 1737 59br Udo Schmidt/Getty Images 60br Library of Congress, Washington, D.C. 61 Down House, Kent 62al Library of Congress, Washington, D.C. 62br British Library, London 63al from John Gould, *The Zoology of the Voyage of H.M.S. Beagle*, 1845 63ar Matthew Field (www.photography.mattfield.com) 63br Stephen Dalton/Minden Pictures/Corbis 64al from *The London Sketch Book*, 1874 64ar Kjersti Joergensen/Shutterstock.com 64bl Stu Porter/Shutterstock.com 65bl Royal College of Surgeons/Eileen Tweedy/The Art Archive 65br Shutterstock.com 66br Smithsonian Institution, Washington, D.C. 67, 68al from Richard Owen, *Memoirs on the Extinct Wingless Birds of New Zealand*, Vol. 2, 1879 68bl George Edward Lodge 68br Roberto Herrett/Loop Images/Corbis 69al Bill Varie/Corbis 69ac Natural History Museum, London 69ar Library of Congress, Washington, D.C. 69cr INTERFOTO/Alamy 69br British Museum, London 70br, 71, 72al, 72c Alfred-Wegener-Institut, Bremerhaven 72ac Sihasak Prachum/Shutterstock.com 73cr Shutterstock.com 73bl Hervas Bengochea/Shutterstock.com 73br Burke Museum of Natural History and Culture, Washington, D.C. 74br Biblioteka Narodowa, Warsaw 75 National Geographic Society/Corbis 76al Bibliothèque Nationale de France, Paris 76ar British Library, London 76cl Shutterstock.com 76bl Szczebrzeszynski 77al Nicolaus Copernicus Museum, Frombork/Bridgeman Art Library 77br Marcin Linfernum/Shutterstock.com 78br from Galileo Galilei, *Istoria e Dimostrazioni intorno alle macchie solari*, 1613 79 National Geographic Society/Corbis 80al from Galileo Galilei, *Sidereus Nuncius*, 1610 80bl Museo della Scienza, Florence 80br SOHO (ESA & NASA) 81al Scala Archives 81r DLR/JPL/NASA 82bl Alan Bean (www.alanbeangallery.com) 82br Museo della Scienza, Florence/Scala Archives 83al Katarina Jankovic 83ar Museo dell Scienza, Florence 83br from Galileo Galilei, *Tractatus de Proportionum instrumento*, 1635 84br Library of Congress, Washington, D.C. 85 Huntington Library/SuperStock 86ar Margaret Bourke-White/Time Life Pictures/Getty Images 86bl Huntington Library/SuperStock 87ar George Grantham Bain Collection/Library of Congress, Washington, D.C. 87cr iStockphoto/Thinkstock.com 87bl Thomas M. Brown, Charles W. Bowers, Randy A. Kimble, Allen V. Sweigart (NASA Goddard Space Flight Center) and Henry C. Ferguson (Space Telescope Science Institute)/NASA 87br Huntington Library/SuperStock 88al Library of Congress, Washington, D.C. 88ar P. Knezek (WIYN)/NASA, ESA, and The Hubble Heritage Team (STScI/AURA) 89ar NASA & ESA 89cr J. Hester and P. Scowen (Arizona State University)/NASA, ESA, STScI 89bl NASA 89br N. Smith (University of California, Berkeley), and The Hubble Heritage Team (STScI/AURA/NASA & ESA) 90br, 91, 92al, 92bl Archives Georges Lemaître, Université catholique de Louvain, Centre de recherche sur le Terre et le climat G. Lemaître, Louvain-la-Neuve, Belgium 92ar G. Illingworth, D. Magee, and P. Oesch (University of California, Santa Cruz), R. Bouwens (Leiden University), and the HUDF09 Team/NASA & ESA 93ar Private Collection 93bl Archives Georges Lemaître, Université catholique de Louvain, Centre de recherche sur le Terre et le climat G. Lemaître, Louvain-la-Neuve, Belgium 93br Stockbyte/Thinkstock.com

On the cover

Front, clockwise from top left: Diagram of the Displacement of the Earth by the Precession of the Equinoxes, Camille Flammarion, *Popular Astronomy*, London 1894; early print of an Armillary Sphere, courtesy www.thegraphicsfairy.com; engraving of a microscope from an 1890s farm magazine, courtesy www.thegraphicsfairy.com; non-Steampunk telescoping india-rubber screw, invented by Trauggott Beek of Newark, N.J., *Scientific American*, May 1877, issue 18. *Back:* Choreutoscope, invented by L.S. Beale in 1866.

On page 2

Hubble Space Telescope photo of an extremely hot and bright star.

Eureka! © 2014 Thames & Hudson Ltd, London

Additional text for Eureka! was provided by Clive Gifford on pages: 12, 14–16, 66, 68–69 and 78. Designed by Karen Wilks

First published in 2014 in hardcover in the United States of America by Thames & Hudson Inc., 500 Fifth Avenue, New York, New York 10110

thamesandhudsonusa.com

First paperback edition 2016

Library of Congress Catalog Card Number 2013948277

ISBN 978-0-500-29227-3

Manufactured in China by Imago